T0013236

ACCOUNTING 101

FROM **CALCULATING REVENUES** AND **PROFITS** TO **DETERMINING ASSETS** AND **LIABILITIES**, AN ESSENTIAL GUIDE TO **ACCOUNTING BASICS**

MICHELE CAGAN, CPA, Author of *Investing 101*

Adams Media
New York   London   Toronto   Sydney   New Delhi

Adams Media
An Imprint of Simon & Schuster, Inc.
100 Technology Center Drive
Stoughton, MA 02072

First Adams Media hardcover edition MAY 2017

ADAMS MEDIA and colophon are trademarks of Simon and Schuster.

For information about special discounts for bulk purchases, please contact Simon & Schuster Special Sales at 1-866-506-1949 or business@simonandschuster.com.

The Simon & Schuster Speakers Bureau can bring authors to your live event. For more information or to book an event contact the Simon & Schuster Speakers Bureau at 1-866-248-3049 or visit our website at www.simonspeakers.com.

Manufactured in the United States of America

8 2024

Library of Congress Cataloging-in-Publication Data has been applied for.

ISBN 978-1-5072-0292-0
ISBN 978-1-5072-0293-7 (ebook)

Contains material adapted from the following title published by Adams Media, an Imprint of Simon & Schuster, Inc.: *The Everything® Accounting Book* by Michele Cagan, CPA, copyright © 2007, ISBN 978-1-59337-718-2.

DEDICATION

To my dad, whose path I followed to success. I miss you.

CONTENTS

CONTENTS

CHAPTER 6
FINANCIAL STATEMENTS 206

CHAPTER 7
ACCOUNTING MOVES FORWARD 234

INTRODUCTION

You may not realize it, but accounting is a huge part of your life. If you bought this book, accounting was involved. If you grabbed a latte at Starbucks this morning, accounting was involved. If your grandmother sent you a birthday card with a $20 bill inside, accounting was involved. In fact, accounting kicks in every time you buy or sell something, pay a bill, get a paycheck, or check your bank balance. However money factors into your life, accounting helps put it in perspective. And whether you're interested in accounting for yourself, your business, or as a high-paying, in-demand career, *Accounting 101* will get you started.

And contrary to the widely held belief that accountants have mind-numbingly boring jobs, accounting is truly one of the most fascinating careers in the world. Here you'll learn about everything from how the terrified ancient bookkeepers kept tallies for the pharaohs to the way today's cutting-edge technology is changing the way we look at money. You'll also see how these revolutionary advances in technology have truly taken accountants away from their adding machines and endless strings of numbers, and brought them into the center of the everyday fray of running a business. Now, along with doing taxes and auditing financial statements, accounting careers include working at the FBI, developing environmental outreach plans, and steering international corporate finances.

Those leaps in technology that have brought accountants into the limelight have brought accounting closer to you, as well. On your phone you may have a budgeting app or an app that you use to track your investments. If you own a small business, you may have apps that let you take payments from customers, organize your expenses, or even update the company books on your phone while you sip a latte. Maybe you even update your numbers in the cloud or file your taxes on your smartphone. Regardless, today's technology will keep advancing—and the future of accounting looks amazingly promising.

Put aside your preset ideas about accountants and accounting, because here you'll find numerous entries that tell you all you need to know about the history of accounting, the exciting career paths accountants can take, the difference between debits and credits, how to read corporate financial statements before you invest, and some of the most innovative personal and business accounting apps available. So fire up your calculators because *Accounting 101* is going to balance your books—and more!

Chapter 1

The Business of Accounting

Accounting is known as "the language of finance." This ancient communication decodes the mysteries of money, translating complex financial concepts into clear, bottom-line numbers that anyone can use. And since we're all interested in money, accounting filters into everyone's life in one way or another.

For as long as people have stored food, or traded spears for pelts, they've figured out some way to account for it. Then currency came along, which made accounting both easier and more difficult: easier because there was now a concrete way to value things, harder because trading (and the results of trading, like infrastructure and taxes) became much more complex. Despite how complicated businesses and personal finances have become, accounting continues to bring order and comparability to the chaos.

With clear record keeping and reporting rules to follow, accounting unites governments, businesses, and citizens in an economy, and keeps both the relevant information and the money flowing. Without it, we couldn't save or invest, we couldn't borrow money to buy our homes, and we couldn't grab cash out of an ATM.

In this chapter, you'll meet all the different people who use accounting information, why they need it, and what they do with it; and that all starts with you and your personal finances. So let's take a look at the many different ways accounting information affects your life.

WHO USES ACCOUNTING INFORMATION?

Everybody Accounts

Virtually everybody uses accounting information, in both their professional and personal lives. Every bank statement, credit card bill, and rent check is full of accounting information. When you double-check the charges on your bar tab, and tack on a healthy tip, you're using accounting. When you shop on Amazon.com, do your taxes, or apply for a student loan, you are providing accounting information. And that's just the everyday-life way you use accounting.

On the business side, accounting is even more pervasive, and most people use at least some accounting information in their jobs every day. Whether you're ordering office supplies, making change for customers, or printing the payroll checks, you are dealing with accounting information.

All of these small pieces of accounting data add up to the big picture of how your household or your company is faring financially. Insiders like heads of households and business owners use this big-picture information to keep finances on track and in the black, which makes sense. After all, when you're the one in charge of the money, you need to know how much you have, how much you owe, and where your money is going.

In addition to you, a lot of other people may want to see how you or your business is doing financially. If you have a business, those people could include employees who need to track particular numbers to get their jobs done and the company accountant who needs numbers in order to prepare reports and help with budget forecasting. This list of outside users is long, varied, and includes:

- Loan officers, for everything from mortgages to student loans to business lines of credit
- Federal, state, and local tax authorities
- Anyone who might offer credit to you or your business
- Potential and existing investors, whether you use crowdfunding or launch a corporate IPO (initial public offering)

These different outside users all have their own reasons for wanting to see accounting numbers. For example, a mortgage lender wants to see that you have saved enough cash for a down payment, aren't drowning in debt, and have a steady source of sustainable income. A tax authority like the IRS looks to make sure that you haven't miscalculated your taxable income or your income tax bill. Creditors look for a lot of the same things that bankers want to see, especially the part where you have a reliable stream of cash coming in. Investors want to feel confident that you manage your resources well, so they'll eventually see healthy returns.

EVERYONE WANTS SOMETHING DIFFERENT

While all of these outside users of your accounting information want to take in-depth looks at your financial status, there's a catch. They don't all need the same information, and they probably won't all want it in the same format.

When you're looking over family finances or the financial picture of your own company, you'll want to see a lot more detail than you would be willing to show outsiders. For example, you might look through your check register and all your credit card statements when figuring out possible deductions for your tax return, but you wouldn't want the IRS looking at those individual line items. That information—like whether you bought books from Amazon.com or subscribe to a video streaming service like Netflix—wouldn't help the IRS determine whether you figured out the right tax payment.

And in your business, while you would report your total sales on your tax return, you wouldn't send the tax authorities a complete breakdown of which customers bought what. Knowing whether your local customers bought more paper products or cleaning products, for example, wouldn't help the state sales tax authority double-check your calculations. But that kind of detailed information could help you figure out things such as whether you're overstocking cleaning products, or whether your company is relying too heavily on sales to a single customer.

GIVE THEM WHAT THEY WANT

We have established that you may have a lot of different people asking to see your personal or business financial statements, and that they may all want to see something different. So what do you do? First, look at who's doing the asking. If it's a tax authority, like the IRS, you have to provide them with the numbers in the format requested. For example, you have to report your income tax on Form 1040; you can't simply send them a printout of numbers from your paystub. The same goes for loan officers: These professionals may look at hundreds of financial statements every week, and they need them to be consistent.

Their needs matter to you as well. If you don't send in the right tax forms to the IRS, you could be subjected to fines, penalties, and interest. Worse, you could be called in for an audit. And if you give your loan officer something other than what he's asked for, you might not get the money you need from him. Even though your numbers look the same regardless of what form they're on, the order and placement can be crucial to the person requesting the information.

Only Answer What You're Asked

If you fill out your own tax forms, a good rule to remember is this: Don't supply more information than the forms ask for. Fill in all the requested numbers, then stop. Don't explain, and don't add details. When you include extra information, you could be flagging your return for audit. Audits aren't necessarily bad—they could show you did everything correctly—but they're generally not pleasant.

TWO SETS OF BOOKS

You may have heard the phrase "two sets of books," often in the context of a law enforcement agent and an arrest warrant. Two sets of books is most often talked about in connection with companies, and their use is more common than you might expect. The truth is that many companies keep one set of books for tax purposes, and another for everyday in-house accounting. Of course, today these "books" are really made up of computer programs, but the same idea holds true.

Why would any business owner bother with that? There are two main reasons.

1. First, computerization has made it incredibly easy to track numbers in multiple ways.
2. Second, what makes sense for taxes, namely minimizing the tax bill, may not make sense for other reasons, like reporting income to investors or trying to borrow money.

In each case, tracking numbers differently for different purposes is perfectly legal, as long as acceptable standards are followed.

For tax purposes, you have to follow IRS requirements, even when they don't make perfect sense for your business. Even some flexible areas, such as certain types of expense calculations, may work differently for in-house purposes (the company's "internal" books), public relations purposes (such as what might appear in a corporate annual report), and tax purposes (meaning what shows up on the tax return). For internal purposes, you may want to use the most realistic numbers, even if those would leave you with a bigger tax burden. Although, when it comes to income taxes, everyone wants to show the lowest possible income because that means the lowest possible tax bill.

While keeping two sets of books can be useful, for most small businesses it's just much simpler to track primarily one set of numbers to avoid confusion. Since everyone has to do things certain ways to comply with IRS requirements, it's easiest to use only those figures for everything. If you decide you'd like to see how things would have worked out if you had used a second set of numbers (a different inventory measurement calculation, for example), you can always figure that out on the side.

ACCOUNTING IS MORE THAN NUMBERS

Paint a Picture with Money

When you think "accounting," you probably picture a report filled with numbers. After all, that's where accounting always starts. When you dig a little deeper, though, you'll see that those numbers only set the foundation for what accounting really is: a way to analyze and make sense of an endless stream of information so that we can make well-informed decisions.

The truth is, numbers without context don't mean much at all. For example, knowing a company had $44 million in sales sounds amazing—at least at first glance. While that single figure might give the impression that the company is successful, the reality might be quite different. That sales number could be down $20 million from last year, possibly indicating that the company's products have fallen out of favor. Or that robust-sounding sales figure could have still resulted in an overall loss for the company; if their costs and expenses exceeded $44 million, the company would have sustained a net loss for the year. There are literally dozens of scenarios where $44 million of revenues don't translate to a successful company— and that's where accounting comes in.

Accounting squirms its way into your personal life, too, and just like with businesses, it's not just about spreadsheets and reports full of numbers. From clipping coupons to saving for a family vacation to stopping for a latte on the way to work, these numbers touch almost everything in your life, every day. There's a more formal side to accounting in personal matters, too. You'll see this side when you:

- Apply for student loans
- Put a percentage of your paycheck in a 401(k) plan
- Do your income taxes
- Create a family budget

All of these activities intimately involve accounting.

LIVING A FINANCIAL LIFE

From the time you started getting an allowance as a kid, accounting became a part of your life. Whether you were an instant spender or a long-term saver, you kept track of your money and what you bought with it. As you got older and scored your first paying job (babysitting, shoveling snow, or bussing tables in a pizza joint), your relationship with accounting began to evolve, getting more sophisticated over time.

For many people, their first real glimpse into the complexity of finances (at least outside of a classroom) came when it was time to pay for college. Putting together all the data for student loans, grants, or scholarship applications involves gathering and organizing financial information, then reporting that information in a prescribed form—the backbone of accounting work. Getting a job, a credit card, a car, and housing likely took your finances to another level. Money flowing in different directions calls for better organization and tracking: You need to know how much money is *really* available to cover your bills, and that amount may not match the current balance of your checking account.

Once past the living paycheck-to-paycheck phase, savings begins in earnest, and in several different ways. In the short term, emergency savings plays the most prominent role. Then there's planning for the future, things like saving for a down payment on your first house, starting a retirement plan, and opening a college fund for your kids. To meet your goals, you need to know where your finances stand today, and what you hope they'll look like in the future. All of that calls for a basic working knowledge of accounting. And bolstered by that knowledge, you can more easily join the growing ranks of independent business owners, and strike out on your own.

STARTING A BUSINESS

If you have an entrepreneurial spirit, you're not alone. According to the U.S. Small Business Administration, there are 28.8 million small businesses that help keep the American economy afloat—and, for all of these businesses, accounting is necessary from Day 1. It's true! As soon as you begin to plan your business launch, accounting takes center stage. The framework for every small business startup is a thorough business plan, complete with an honest assessment of assets, a realistic view of expectations, and pro forma financial statements (meaning statements based on those expectations rather than actual historical numbers, also called projections).

You're a Business

If you moonlight, freelance, or consult for a fee rather than a paycheck, you're a business. That means you'll have business expenses to deduct directly from your income. When you're a business, all of the money you spend to make money (like phone and Internet service) reduces the impending tax burden of all the income you earned.

Once the business is up and running, you need to keep accounting at the forefront. Yes, the day-to-day responsibilities can result in overlooked bookkeeping tasks, but that work must be completed and kept current if the business has any chance of success. Without up-to-date accounting, you can't plan properly for the future of your company, or analyze its wins and losses. The story of your business—and whether or not it will live happily ever after—depends on accounting.

Top Ten Small Business Accounting Mistakes

Unfortunately, a lot of small business owners leave accounting issues to the side, figuring they'll get it all done eventually—or at least trust that their accountant will take care of things at the end of the year. While the daily bookkeeping tasks and financial analysis may not seem interesting, they tell you things you really need to know, like whether you're charging enough for your services or how many customers owe you money. By avoiding the numbers, you could be putting your company in jeopardy. Don't fall into the same traps that have caused thousands of small businesses to fail. These traps include:

1. **Not knowing your true cash balance:** Due to things like automatic payments, outstanding checks, and bank charges, money that appears in your cash drawer and your checking account may already be spent.
2. **Extending credit without checking credit:** Until you collect some basic credit information about a customer, don't make on-account sales, where your company extends credit (rather than getting paid immediately with cash or credit card) and bills the customer later. A sale isn't much good if your company never gets paid.

3. **Mistaking profits for cash:** When your company makes a lot of credit (or on-account) sales, your company can post big profits without seeing any cash. When you make a sale, it counts toward revenue and profits, even if your company hasn't yet gotten paid by the customer. But you can't pay your bills with profits; you can only pay them with cash.

4. **Paying bills too soon:** If your vendors give you 30 days to pay them, take it. Unless you get a discount for paying early, paying your bills only when they're due improves your company's cash flow. Because cash is so precious to new and small business owners, having as much easily available cash as possible can help you stay solvent, especially when unexpected expenses come up.

5. **Avoiding bookkeeping tasks:** Not recording transactions regularly can leave you with a mountain of bookkeeping to deal with instead of a molehill. Plus, the time lag can act like a vacuum, where transaction records disappear and the transactions never are recorded.

6. **Not hiring a payroll service:** The minor cost of hiring out this task provides a huge benefit for your company. It can free up your time, and help your company avoid financial penalties from state and federal agencies that go along with late and incorrect payroll tax filings.

7. **Paying accidental dividends:** Every time a corporation owner takes money out of his business, it counts as a dividend (an official distribution from the corporation to the shareholder; all corporation owners are called shareholders). That can lead to a bigger personal income tax bill, because dividends are included in taxable income.

8. **Not keeping personal finances separate from business:** Mixing up business and personal money can cause both

bookkeeping and legal problems. On the bookkeeping side, paying personal expenses with business money causes a dividend or distribution, and that can confuse the accounting entries. On the legal side, mixing the two can take away the personal financial protection gained by incorporating or forming an LLC (both of which are designed to shield your personal money from business lawsuits).

9. **Setting prices too low:** If you don't know your costs before you set product or service prices, you run the risk of losing money on every sale. A simple break-even analysis can help you set prices at a profitable level. For example, if you order fifty clocks to sell in your store, you need to take into account things like sales tax, delivery fees, and overhead expenses related to the clocks to come up with the real, break-even price.

10. **Turning over all the financial stuff to someone else:** Without an intimate knowledge of your company's finances, you can't make successful decisions. Even if you don't want to deal with the daily bookkeeping tasks, look at your financial statements every month so that you can plan for profits and prevent potential problems.

INVESTING YOUR MONEY

Investing, which means putting your money into a company run by someone else, really spurs the need for reliable, consistent accounting information. When you're deciding whether and where to invest, you want a novel's worth of accounting data and analysis; a synopsis put out by the corporation itself will never give the full, true picture of the company's prospects.

In this role, accounting speaks to your future financial health. A corporation will dazzle potential investors with colorful pictures, "heartfelt" statements, and numbers highlighted in the most glowing form possible to attract more money to their coffers. But when you understand the ins and outs of those numbers, and have a real handle on the accounting practices employed by the company, the gloss will lose its sheen and the real story will begin to reveal itself. Sometimes, that story will disclose a company that is really worthy of your trust and your savings; other times, it will expose "creative" accounting, shady business practices, and glaring red flags that signal you should invest somewhere else.

The only way to know whether your investment target is a stud or a dud is to listen to the tale the numbers tell, rather than simply focusing on the figures themselves.

ANCIENT ACCOUNTING

Five Shells for Three Rocks, Please

Archaeologists and historians believe that accounting may have come even before writing. In fact, some believe that primitive writing itself was developed from using marks to keep track of goods stored in ancient warehouses, more than 5,000 years ago. And that makes sense, because from the earliest days of civilization, people engaged in trade.

In Mesopotamia, the "cradle of civilization," ancient scribes recorded commerce activities, like trading wheat or wool for ivory or copper, on thick clay tablets. The Mesopotamians traded with other ancient peoples, including the Phoenicians, a sea-faring civilization that brought goods from faraway lands—exotic spices, brilliant dyes, and precious metals—to the fertile region.

Ancient Money Transfers

Bankers in ancient Greece kept account books detailing their clients' "cash transfers" through other banks in the region. They also loaned money to citizens, and changed money for clients who had currencies from other lands. These practices were a forerunner to the modern international banking system we count on today.

In time, currencies were created, and accounting for trades took on a different tint. Ancient Greek bankers kept detailed records in logbooks. The Romans relied on family patriarchs to account for currency and trade movements. People in Middle

Eastern lands developed rudimentary arithmetic to make sure trades were even-handed, and to track inventory stores and government holdings.

ROYAL TREASURY FINANCED THE PYRAMIDS

In the tomb of King Scorpion I of ancient Egypt, archaeologists found something unexpected: the roots of accounting. Attached to bags of linen and oils were "tags" made of bone, each inscribed with inventory marks. Bookkeepers of that ancient culture painstakingly recorded the contents of royal storehouses, making sure every piece of inventory was accounted for accurately. When they got even a single piece of information wrong, a harsh penalty—mutilation or death—was applied.

Ancient Takeout

Though it originated in China (reportedly in or around 3000 B.C.), the abacus was a favored counting tool among ancient Egyptians. An abacus (sometimes called a counting frame) consists of a series of rods or wires set in a rectangular frame; users slide beads up and down the rods to make simple mathematical calculations.

As Egyptian society grew more complex, so did the record keeping. As the value of labor was recognized, simple counting no longer worked to capture costs, so the Egyptians had to come up with a way to account for effort and results. That led to more sophisticated systems for keeping track of the royal wealth, as bookkeepers were expected to measure the royal capital (total wealth), as well as track agricultural and building projects, including the great pyramids.

These new accounting needs of ancient Egyptian rulers resulted in the use of papyrus, a sort of paper made from reeds, to permanently record information. Among the public records were tax receipts, tribute payments (to the pharaoh from nearby kingdoms), and royal inventory.

100 EGGS FOR A DINING TABLE

Accounting was also progressing in other parts of the world, including the way people recorded their business dealings. During the Middle Ages, before money began to circulate in Europe, people used a barter and trade system to get what they needed. And out of this barter and trade system, the need for written record keeping emerged, with each person detailing his side of the agreement. Unlike modern accounting ledgers that are filled with unending columns and rows of numbers, these books contained colorful narratives describing trades. For example, a farmer's ledger might read like this:

Thursday, 15 March: I provided Josiah Greenwood five chickens today in exchange for ten sacks of grain.
Tuesday, 24 April: Henry Smith agreed to build for me a six-foot dining table in exchange for 100 eggs, to be delivered to him once the table is completed. I will deliver 10 eggs per week for 10 weeks once it is finished.

Monday, 7 June: I agreed to supply 20 eggs per week to William Hart in exchange for 2 gallons of milk per week. This agreement will last for one year from today.

Since some of the bargains, such as those used in this example, would be fulfilled long after the agreements were made, these books also served as proof of the trades when disagreements landed people in front of magistrates. Those very detailed descriptions also helped people keep track of their goods or services, and plan ahead for lean times.

CURRENCY AND COMPUTATIONS

When currency began to make its way into trading systems, everything changed. Recordkeeping now focused sharply on numbers. Merchants and craftsmen started to focus on making profits and building wealth instead of simply trading what they had for what they needed. Bookkeepers came back into fashion, as many successful traders were not adept at mathematics. Instead of struggling with the numbers themselves, the bookkeepers that the merchants hired began to track how much the merchants owed, how much was owed to them, and how much they had stored.

The ledgers themselves looked somewhat similar to those that came before, with one big addition: a special column for numbers. Now every trade came with a price tag, either money going out or coming in. Each narrative description was therefore followed by a dollar amount (based on the local currency).

Now that same farmer's ledger might read like this:

LEDGER		
DATE	DESCRIPTION	AMOUNT
Thursday, 15 March	sold 5 chickens	+$15
Thursday, 15 March	bought 10 sacks of grain	−$15
Tuesday, 24 April	bought dining table	−$100
Tuesday, 24 April	sold 100 eggs	+$100
Monday, 7 June	sold 20 eggs	+$10
Monday, 7 June	bought 2 gallons of milk	−$10

Merchants and tradesmen would simply tell their bookkeepers about any deals they had made that day. With that information, the bookkeeper created a description of the trade, and then figured out whether to add or subtract money from the ledger. At the end of the month, the bookkeeper would tally all of the entries from that month—a very time-consuming project, as each transaction caused at least two entries in the ledger—and calculate whether there was a profit or loss for the merchant. Luckily, that tiresome method of bookkeeping would soon change.

AN ITALIAN FRIAR CHANGES EVERYTHING

Back in the late fifteenth century, a charismatic Italian friar named Luca Pacioli forever changed the face of accounting, in ways that we still use today. Pacioli began tutoring merchants' sons on mathematics when he was still a teenager. From there he joined the Franciscan order, becoming a friar. But it was his love and deep understanding of mathematics that led him to the first chair in mathematics at the prestigious University of Perugia in the subject.

In the accounting world, Pacioli is still highly revered for his detailed description of double-entry accounting (where all parts of a transaction are recorded in a single accounting entry), a system that has stood through the centuries. This description was included in his revolutionary book, *Summa de Arithmetica, Geometria, Proportioni et Proportionalita*. In addition to being a primer on debits and credits (crucial components of accounting entries that determine whether account balances will be increased or decreased), which are the building blocks that led to modern accounting, this book explains accounting procedures, such as the proper use of ledgers and journals, in great detail. Using this streamlined method, that farmer's ledger might look something like this:

DATE	DESCRIPTION	AMOUNT	DEBIT ACCOUNT	CREDIT ACCOUNT
Thursday, 15 March	sold 5 chickens	$15	Cash	Sales
Thursday, 15 March	bought 10 sacks of grain	$15	Grain	Cash
Tuesday, 24 April	bought dining table	$100	Furniture	Cash
Tuesday, 24 April	sold 100 eggs	$100	Cash	Sales
Monday, 7 June	sold 20 eggs	$10	Cash	Sales
Monday, 7 June	bought 2 gallons of milk	$10	Milk	Cash

This seminal work also includes topics such as the accounting cycle, ethics in accounting, and the then revolutionary idea that debits had to equal credits before the bookkeeper's workday was done. With that, it is no wonder Pacioli was dubbed the "Father of Modern Accounting."

MODERN ACCOUNTING

From Coins to Corporate Shares

Business, in terms of both commerce and trade, began to flourish as the Industrial Revolution spread throughout Europe, particularly in Great Britain. This combination prompted the need for more rigorous and advanced accounting systems and procedures. Around that time (the early 1600s), the first corporations were born, calling for additional changes and advancements. Accounting had been dragged into the modern age, and it was time for a complete makeover.

Unlike the simple transactions of the past, new manufacturing and factory-based businesses called for more complex cost accounting (figuring out exactly how much it cost to make a product). Basic materials were now being transformed into completely different goods, and complete inventories were required every step of the way. Figuring out cost and profits became complicated, and the need for accurate tracking increased.

With the advent of this new corporate structure, where the shareholders (owners) rarely took part in everyday operations, for the first time in history there was distance between a company and its owners. With this new business structure, the owners might never even see the company, its workers, its managers, its products, or even its other owners. The corporation itself was a stand-alone entity (at least for legal and financial purposes), regardless of who created the business or got it up and running. Those owners were very interested in what was going on behind the business doors, and they relied on accountants to fill them in on the financial picture. That led to more sophisticated reporting requirements, and a lot of new rules and regulations.

CORPORATIONS CHANGE ACCOUNTING

With the rise of corporations, the more basic chores of bookkeeping evolved into the complex set of rules that govern accounting today. In the earliest days, corporations were hungry to raise capital for startup and expansion. To entice investors, they would spread the word of their plans for profits among friends and family. People, always eager to make a quick buck, threw their money into investments, often blindly trusting others' advice. Then, investing was really gambling: if you got lucky, you would reap profits; if not, you could lose everything, right down to the shirt on your back.

As the investing public began to grow wary, the money stream began to dry up. So corporations started publishing financial statements that showed how well they were doing. Still, investors did not have complete trust in those corporate numbers, and that gave rise to a new field within accounting. Now, instead of just compiling the numbers into readable reports, accountants were called upon to independently review those numbers—and the profession began to grow in earnest.

THE RAILROAD POWERS CHANGE

Perhaps even more transformative in the field of accounting than the creation of corporations was the U.S. railroad, which in the early 1800s had an enormous impact on new investors and the way business was conducted. In order to move people and goods to far-off destinations and make a profit along the way, the railroads needed detailed financial information. The industry was fueled by money, and competition was fierce.

The railroad barons turned to accountants for cost reports, competitive fare setting, expansion estimates, operating ratios, and financial statements. Armed with that information, they could make better decisions about routes, rates, and revenue streams.

As the railroads made the country smaller, interstate trade expanded dramatically. Transactions that had previously taken weeks or months to settle now took only days or hours. The speed of business increased, along with the number of deals that were made. Investors were intrigued by the potential for faster profits, and they called on accountants to fill in information gaps.

A WAR, A CRASH, AND A GOVERNMENT RESPONSE

The accounting profession was officially established in the United States in 1896, and the title of CPA (certified public accountant) was born. Those early CPAs faced strict licensing requirements, including experience and examination, to ensure they could keep up with the increasing demand for financial information. That recognition came at the perfect time, because just thirteen years later, Congress passed the 16th Amendment, which allowed Uncle Sam to officially levy income taxes on all Americans.

World War I

At first, the tax was relatively low, more of a token payment. But then World War I struck, and the federal income tax became the centerpiece of the government's revenue agenda. As the country became enmeshed in the war, rates climbed, and the graduated tax rates (where different income levels are subject to different tax rates) debuted, with the top-tier rate an astonishing 63 percent. Around the same time, in 1917, Congress created a levy on corporations, taxing all profits over a "reasonable" rate of return. All of these changes placed an overwhelming burden on the struggling Bureau of Internal Revenue, because suddenly there were many more taxpayers, but the government was pleased to see its coffers overflowing, and kept all the taxes in force. These new collection efforts brought a lot of work to accountants, and more was about to come.

Uncle Sam Wants More Money

According to the Tax History Project, income taxes made up about 16 percent of federal revenue in 1916. That portion spiked up as high as 58 percent between 1917 and 1920. Today, income taxes make up 46.2 percent of the total federal revenue each year.

A Spike and Then a Crash

The demand for accountants held steady for a while after the income tax–related spike, prior to 1920. After emerging victorious from World War I, Americans were confident and optimistic, and they poured all that belief into the stock market without a thought of the risk, even though the vast majority of investors had no inkling of how the market worked. That enthusiasm mixed with a lot of money, and swindlers came out in force to artificially drive up stock prices for their own gain. But that upward momentum couldn't be sustained, and on October 29, 1929, the stock market crashed, not to fully recover for many years.

After the Great Depression wiped out fortunes across the country, the government and the people began calling for more corporate accountability, and soon the U.S. government began passing laws, as part of President Roosevelt's New Deal, to calm investors and restore confidence in the stock market.

ACCOUNTING RULES

Follow the Numbers to the Letter

The world of accounting is governed by an abundance of rules, some broad in scope and others detailed down to the penny. Throughout history, different societal needs have given rise to new math and new methods that have been built haphazardly on what came before. As different cultures interacted and merged, their often contrasting rules could contradict each other, and so accountants and businesses called for clarification. Over time, accounting rules were systematically organized within countries, giving clear guidance to accounting, tax, and financial professionals.

The first official rules for accounting in the United States came from the Securities and Exchange Commission, commonly called the SEC, and didn't stop there.

THE SEC CREATES MORE WORK FOR ACCOUNTANTS

When America got wise to the widespread financial fraud that had brought on the Great Depression, lawmakers knew they needed to take serious steps. So in 1934, they created the SEC to restore confidence in the stock market, as well as enforce new rules meant to regulate public corporations and clamp down on illegal financial activity. To that end, the government mandates that every corporation whose stock trades in the United States has to be registered with the SEC, and that these corporations must disclose specific financial information to the public, including independently audited financial statements.

Once again, the need for qualified accounting professionals soared. With public corporations now legally obligated to hire CPAs, interest in the profession grew. And with so much distrust of corporations among investors, people placed their faith in these independent auditors to root out deception and fraud.

THE FINANCIAL ACCOUNTING STANDARDS BOARD

In 1973, the Financial Accounting Standards Board, or FASB (pronounced "fazz-bee"), was born. This private sector group (as opposed to government entity) sets the comprehensive standards, rules, and guidelines that drive the accounting industry. Of course, they do this within the framework of SEC regulations, but since not all companies are corporations, SEC rules don't always apply.

The Government Has GASB

While private sector accountants are ruled by FASB, accountants working for the federal government are held to a different set of standards known as GASB ("gazz-bee"), where the G stands for *Government*.

FASB guidance is designed to make sure investors (along with other financial report users) are given useful, transparent information that accurately represents the financial health of a company—not just the information a company's management wants to share. In addition, since their rules apply to all types of companies, these uniform standards work across all kinds of different financial markets.

FINANCIAL SCANDALS YIELD NEW REGULATIONS

The most recent laws to rock the accounting profession rose up out of scandal and a devastating impact on the American economy. Ironically, these limiting regulations had the effect of creating more work for accountants, and boosting demand for their top-line services.

After the WorldCom, Tyco, and Enron scandals of 2000–2002, the U.S. Congress created and passed the Sarbanes-Oxley Act (commonly known as SOX) in 2002. That legislation placed much stricter regulations on accounting firms and their consulting services as a way to better protect the investing public from fraudulent corporate financial activity through financial transparency, particularly ensuring that the accountants wouldn't be in on the fraud (as was the case with Enron's accounting firm, Arthur Andersen, which signed off on their fraudulent filings).

The three most impactful provisions of SOX involve personal responsibility and corporate integrity:

1. **Section 302** calls for the senior management of a corporation to attest to the accuracy of the financial statements, meaning the CEO (chief executive officer) and CFO (chief financial officer) now bear personal responsibility for the numbers in those reports.

2. **Section 404** demands creating and maintaining strict internal controls, which includes having an impressive internal audit team.
3. **Section 802** spells out which accountant records need to be kept and for how long, to make sure records are not destroyed or fraudulently fabricated.

Equally important, according to TITLE II—Auditor Independence, external accountants are not allowed to audit the books for a company they also did management or consulting work for, requiring corporations to hire two separate firms for those tasks.

All of these very strict guidelines will help protect investors from "creative" accounting practices that *appear* to follow the basic rules of accounting, known as GAAP.

GENERALLY ACCEPTED ACCOUNTING PRINCIPLES

Mind the GAAP

In the United States, the current prevailing set of rules guiding financial reporting is known as GAAP (pronounced "gap"), which stands for Generally Accepted Accounting Principles. The main goal of GAAP is the creation of consistent financial statements year after year, giving investors a clearer picture of a company's financial situation. All publicly traded companies must provide yearly audited financial statements prepared in accordance with GAAP.

The purpose of GAAP is to make sure that the information provided in financial statements is relevant, reliable, comparable, and consistent:

- **Relevant** means that numbers provide the information that a reasonable person would need to see in order to make a smart investment decision.
- **Reliable** means that the information can be verified as accurate by an independent third party.
- **Comparable** means that this company's financial statements contain the same information as others in the same industry.
- **Consistent** means that the numbers on the statements are calculated the same way, based on the same accounting estimates and principles used in prior years.

These characteristics are particularly critical for the investors in publicly held corporations, because they use this information to make sound investment decisions. Without GAAP, misinformation can lead investors to unwittingly purchase dodgy investments.

THE BASIC PRINCIPLES

There are a lot of detailed rules and guidelines spelling out exactly how to account for financial transactions. However, when it comes to GAAP, there are ten important guiding principles that set the framework for virtually all things accounting:

1. **Full disclosure**, the most important principle, calls for anything—pending lawsuits, expected changes in law, incomplete transactions, and the like—that might have an impact on financial statements to be revealed and reported.
2. The **economic entity assumption** says that each company (or person, or government entity) has a distinct and unique identity, and must maintain its own separate accounting records.
3. The **monetary unit assumption** means that all transactions can be expressed in terms of money, and that the monetary unit selected (whether it's the U.S. dollar or the Japanese yen) is stable and secure.
4. **Revenue recognition** requires that revenues must be counted when they're earned, regardless of when actual money changes hands.
5. The **matching principle** states that expenses must be reported in the same period as the revenue they're related to, again regardless of when money changes hands.
6. The **going concern principle** is based on the idea that, at least in regard to accounting for and the reporting of

financial statement information, the economic entity will exist indefinitely.

7. The **time period** speaks to discrete time intervals (months, quarters, years, or fiscal years, for example) that must be spelled out on financial statements.

8. **Cost principle** requires that values reported on financial statements refer to historical cost, which is the actual amount paid rather than current market value or value adjusted for inflation.

9. **Materiality** speaks to the relative importance of errors or misstatements, and how much they would affect the people who rely on the accuracy of the financial statements.

10. **Conservatism** calls for the financial statements to represent the most conservative numbers possible, and requires likely liabilities and expenses to be recorded right away (even if they may not occur) and revenues to be recognized only when they're earned.

WHEN THINGS CHANGE

Though a core tenet in accounting calls for consistency across financial statements, changes happen. How these changes are dealt with is one place where virtually all standard-setting boards agree. There are two sweeping changes that impact past, current, and future financial statements:

1. Changes in accounting estimates
2. Changes in accounting principles

Keep in mind that these changes have nothing to do with error corrections, like fixing math mistakes or adjusting improperly booked entries (crediting the office supplies account instead of the office furniture account, for example) even if they might look that way to uninitiated investors.

Change in Accounting Estimates

A change in accounting estimates occurs when a company recalculates a number or percentage they've been using in their financial statement calculations. Sometimes, accountants use estimates to record values they can't quite pin down, using the best information they can gather at the time. Values commonly estimated in the accounting world include things like how long a fixed asset, such as property or equipment, might last or the costs a company may face related to warranty expense on a new product. When an estimate turns out to be too far off the mark, the accountants can revise it. If the impact of changing the estimate is considered immaterial, there's nothing more for the accountant to do. However, if it affects multiple accounting periods, the change, particularly the impact on net income, has to be disclosed in the company's financial statements.

Accounting Periods Stop Time

An accounting period covers a specific amount of time—a month, a quarter, a year—for tracking transactions, and that period must be clearly stated on financial statements. For example, if you looked at annual financial statements, the related accounting period would be one year, indicated as "for the year ending December 21, 2016."

Change in Accounting Principles

A change in accounting principle takes place when a company's financial managers decide to switch the method they've used in the past to calculate numbers on their financial statements. For example, changing the method used to value inventory would be a change in accounting principle. As long as the change is acceptable under GAAP or IFRS (International Financial Reporting Standards, a worldwide set of accounting guidelines), it is perfectly allowable, provided that the company properly discloses the impact of the change. To do this, the company has to retroactively apply that change to all of its earlier reporting periods, as if that's how they'd been doing things all along. This is known as "restating" the financial statements. In addition, the change has to be fully detailed and disclosed in the footnotes that accompany the financial statements.

MIND THE NON-GAAP

Sometimes, however, using GAAP doesn't paint the truest picture of a company's financial position or the performance of its core business, and in those circumstances, a company might record transactions using non-GAAP methods. For example, GAAP requires one-time expenses linked with restructuring a business to be included in the year-end results, even though that restructuring will impact the company's future; deducting that expense all at once ties it to the year in which it occurred, even though that's not really when the expense is relevant.

Some companies' financial statements may diverge from GAAP in situations like this, which could have a profound effect on how investors view their future prospects. That's especially true for regular-Joe investors (as opposed to institutional or professional investors), who place a lot of stock in bottom-line earnings. While it is legal to use non-GAAP methods and allowed by the SEC, this accounting practice can also be used to distort earnings, showing them in a more favorable light than they'd appear under GAAP. Non-GAAP has no set accounting methods that must be followed, so it's easier to tweak the numbers, and there's little consistency. Furthermore, non-GAAP accounting is not allowed to create a false picture of the company, and its use must be reported to the SEC.

DIFFERENT COUNTRIES, DIFFERENT PRINCIPLES

Historically, countries developed their own versions of acceptable accounting principles as their economies became more sophisticated, similar to GAAP in the United States. The differences in these national systems varied from nuanced to extreme. For example, the way pensions were treated under U.S. GAAP bears no resemblance to how they were accounted for in Asia or Europe. Because of the disparities, international investing was quite confusing and investors looking at companies in different countries struggled to figure out which was the best choice for their portfolios.

On top of that, some countries—particularly those with still-emerging markets—didn't really have any established accounting principles at all. Without experienced accounting professionals in place, there was no one to set the standards, and so they were put together in a piecemeal fashion with different rules being pulled from different countries ahead of them on the industrialization scale.

That hodgepodge collection of rules made for even more investor confusion and skepticism—could any of these financial statements really be reliable?

As global trade and finance increased, so did the need for international accounting standards. This need led to the creation of the independent International Accounting Standards Board, or IASB, in London in 2001. This global group is composed of fifteen members from nine countries, including the United States. IASB works together with its U.S. counterpart, FASB, to establish standardized financial reporting that crosses borders.

The IASB set the International Financial Reporting Standards (IFRS), which are quickly becoming the worldwide standard for preparing financial statements for publicly held companies. Unlike U.S. GAAP, the IFRS takes a principles-based approach (U.S. GAAP is completely rules-focused), which gives accountants more wiggle room when deciding how to approach information presentation. More than 100 countries either allow or require IFRS to be used for publicly held companies, but the United States still isn't completely on board with the conversion. That lack of involvement can make U.S. corporate reports more difficult to decipher by outside investors, and harder for all investors to compare international companies when choosing investments.

TRACKING AND MEASURING SUCCESS

Accounting Insights Bring Success

Whether you're looking at your retirement plan, college savings, or business profits, it's crucial for you to know what the numbers you see actually mean. For example, which is more important: revenues or profits? Do average annual returns really indicate what's going on in your retirement account? Though the answers to these questions may seem simple and obvious, they're not. Knowing the intricacies of the numbers that show up in annual reports and financial statements can better help you meet your goals.

HOW TO SUCCEED IN BUSINESS

When you first dreamed of starting your own business, you may have thought about happy customers, the luxury of being your own boss, or building a nice chunk of wealth for your family. All those things are possible, once your business starts to take off. Getting it to that point, though, means doing something that gives many people queasy stomachs: working with a lot of numbers.

Underneath every business success story—from the tiniest home-based business to the largest *Fortune* 500 corporation—are numbers and reports and some math. Behind many business failures is a failure to work with and understand these numbers. With a working knowledge of the basics, you can avoid that fate and watch your dreams come true.

Accounting provides a comprehensive toolbox designed to help you build your business up from a solid foundation. Starting with a thorough business plan gives you a clear sense of direction, along with a map of potential landmines to avoid and measurable goals to reach. As your business begins to take shape, accounting data helps keep you on course. In the beginning, cash and sales will feel like the most important numbers to watch, but focusing only on those could leave your company vulnerable to failure. Yes, cash and sales are crucial, but so are costs, expenses, and liabilities; if those grow large enough, they can strangle the company's cash, and even robust sales won't be able to revive it.

Tracking all of the numbers, and keeping an eye on changes in the financial statements, is the best way to ensure success. Accounting gives you a way to figure out what those numbers mean in terms of your business, and shows you how they work together to measure your company's financial health. It lets you track all the important numbers, such as cash, sales, and overhead expenses. It helps give you the true measure of how well your business is doing, which could be quite different than how things appear on the surface. If something goes awry, you'll know about it in time to make a course correction. You'll be able to see where you're spending too much, whether your prices need adjusting, which products are the moneymakers, and if your business will really be able to handle its current debt load. All of these factors play into a profitable business. And your accounting records and reports hold all of the pieces you need to operate a successful business.

FOLLOW THE NUMBERS TO PERSONAL SUCCESS

Just like with a business, achieving personal financial success—whatever that means to you—requires that you know exactly how much money you have, how much you owe, and how much you need to meet your goals. This knowledge forms the cornerstone of your plan. You probably deal with a lot of numbers in your personal life: writing rent checks, paying down student loan debt, checking the balance in your 401(k) plan, and so on. Staying on top of your personal finances, from debt to savings to retirement funds, can mean the difference between financial freedom and personal bankruptcy. From this starting point, you can begin to put strategies in place to wipe out your debt and build your fortune.

Financial Priorities

According to a survey by TransAmerica, the top three financial priorities for Americans are saving for retirement, covering basic living expenses, and paying off credit card debt.

Do the Numbers Work?

So how can you tell if your numbers add up? Start by gathering up your most important financial documents: bank statements, last year's tax return, current paystubs, credit card statements, monthly bills, retirement account statement, and investment holdings. Armed with that information, you can make better plans for your financial future.

Some of the most important things to do to get control of your finances include:

- Creating a household budget so you can track where your money is *really* going. This will help make sure you don't run out of money before the end of the month.
- Knowing what you owe so you can take charge of paying down your debt before it balloons out of control. You don't want to end up financially crippled by credit card debt, or the enormous interest charges that can come with it.
- Building emergency savings to cover at least six months of living expenses. You can't predict when an injury will keep you out of work, or a company will downsize, and unexpected occurrences like these can wreak havoc on your finances if you aren't prepared.
- Beginning to fund your retirement today because time really is money. The earlier you start saving, the more your nest egg will grow—even if you stop adding money to it later on.
- Setting up focused savings accounts to fund each of your goals (car, house, tropical beach vacation, and so on). Keeping these funds strictly separated and tracked helps ensure you'll really meet each goal.

Once the foundation of your money management plan is set up, you can spend some time looking at ways to maximize your money. For example, you can take steps to minimize your tax bill and keep more of your paycheck, or start investing some extra cash to earn more than you would from a typical savings account. At this point, whether you're building your business or personal financial plan, you may want to call in an accountant to help you get on track.

HOW ACCOUNTANTS CAN HELP YOU

Call In a Professional

Whether you need help with personal or business finances, a professional accountant can guide you through each step of your financial life. For personal finances, an accountant can help you determine how to pay off student loans, buy your first house, and plan your estate. The same holds true if you're launching a business: An accountant can walk you through a business plan, help you secure financing, assist you in tracking and measuring your company's profitability, and be your ally as you bridge the gap from startup to successful enterprise.

Accountants can also represent you if you're ever called in to the IRS for personal or business reasons, just like you would be represented by a lawyer if you had to go to court. While you are allowed to face the IRS on your own, it's a good idea to have a seasoned professional on your side, someone who knows the ins and outs of tax law, and how to apply the most advantageous rules to your unique circumstances.

MORE THAN JUST TAXES

Tax planning can help you minimize your annual tax bill and avoid potential pitfalls that could lead to penalties and interest charges. Your accountant will be familiar with dozens of deductions and loopholes that you've never heard of, and can help you figure out which ones apply to your situation, saving you potentially hundreds—even thousands—of dollars in taxes. Most people only think about visiting their accountants during tax season.

Swipe Right?

Looking for an easy way to separate business and personal expenses? Ducky, by Swipefin, is an app designed for freelancers, contractors, and entrepreneurs to help them separate expenses on the go. Just swipe right for business transactions; swipe left for personal stuff. It's like Tinder for tax deductions!

But it's important to realize that your accountant is a valuable financial resource who can do so much more than just tally up your taxes. The best accountants can help you dig deeper into your current financial situation, sort out thorny issues like excess debt and out-of-control budgets, and help you attain your personal goals. From buying your first house to paying for college to retiring in luxury, your accountant can guide you through every step along the way.

TAKING CARE OF BUSINESS

If you don't have a background in business accounting or finance, it could be easy for you to get the numbers wrong, or sometimes even overlook certain numbers altogether, which can seriously impair your planning. When you're just starting out in business, having a professional accountant on your team can make your life as an entrepreneur so much simpler. On top of that, an accountant will help you figure out what kind of business structure makes the most sense for your company.

When it comes to setting up your books, getting it right from the start is a must, even if you use the most basic do-it-yourself software package. Trying to change it after the fact can be time-consuming and even more confusing.

Once your business is up and running, you'll find many more reasons to have an accountant. Whether you want a professional to take over the drudgery of bookkeeping tasks, create more useful reports so you can track your success, or go over the numbers with you, an accountant can handle it. She can also help you move your business forward, proposing the most cost-effective plans for next month or next year. Having her available to walk you through the finances frees up your time so that you can focus on the business of running your business.

Not Mixing Business and Personal

While you may be comfortable with the CPA who's been doing your personal taxes, he may not be the best person to deal with your business taxes. The two types are very different, and someone well-versed in personal returns may not have a lot of experience in small business returns. That can lead to an unnecessarily high tax bill on your business income. It's very important to make sure that whoever takes care of your business taxes knows the ins and outs of a business return.

Taxes are an integral part of business, and tax time is more frequent and more complicated for businesses. Whether you're dealing with sales tax, payroll taxes, or income taxes, having an experienced professional deal with the paperwork will remove a huge headache-producer from your life. Plus, in addition to your time savings, you could end up saving money. Tax mistakes can be pretty costly, in part because late filings are subject to fees and fines. Also, professional income tax preparers really know their way around deductions, which can greatly reduce your company's income tax bill.

Whatever stage of business your company is in, getting help from an accounting professional will do just that: help you. Let's take a closer look.

"I Want to Start a Business"

Hundreds of new businesses open every day in the United States, and every year tens of thousands of them fold. A lot of the time, those failures could have been prevented easily with better financial planning and management, two areas where an experienced small business accountant can help. In fact, if you hook up with an accountant during the planning stage, he will be able to point out potential pitfalls before they show up, and help you figure out ways to prevent or deal with them.

If you've started working on a business plan (something no new business should be without), you know there are pages upon pages of numbers involved. When it's your first business plan for your first business, coming up with those numbers can be a daunting task. First, you have to figure out how much it will realistically cost to get your company off the ground, and where that money is coming from. Without enough startup cash, your business may not even make it past the planning stage. Then you have to estimate what your sales and expenses (among other things) will be over the next couple of years. Experienced accountants won't even blink when you ask them to help you come up with these numbers; it's a key part of their job, and they can do so much more. These are some other things that accountants can do for startup businesses:

- Help you choose the best business structure (like corporation or limited liability company [LLC])
- Introduce you to bankers
- Set up your accounting system
- Teach you how to use your accounting system
- Show you different ways to keep initial costs down
- Help you get all the necessary tax ID numbers

Most important, your accountant can guide you through the ins and outs of getting your business off the ground. Bolstered by your accountant's experience, you and your company will have a better chance of success—and then you can start worrying about things like minimizing your tax bill, a very good problem to have.

Corporations and LLCs

Both corporations and LLCs legally shield personal assets from business liabilities, but their accounting set-ups are different. Corporations (which pay their own taxes on company profits) are owned by shareholders, who receive taxable dividends from their shares of corporate profits when they take money out of the business. LLCs are owned by members (similar to partners) who pay tax on their proportional shares of total profits and take money out of the company as nontaxable distributions.

Once Your Company Is Up and Running

After your company has been around for a few months, you will have a better feel for the way your business flows. You'll also know by then which things you like to do yourself, which things you feel you have to do yourself, and which things you cannot wait to pass off to somebody else. A lot of the time, what ends up falling into that last category will be the more routine bookkeeping and paperwork tasks.

Bookkeeping

Once you know how to do bookkeeping tasks, and what the results of the work should look like, you may be ready to stop doing them yourself. If so, then it's the time to consider bringing in a bookkeeper, whether you put one on your regular payroll or just bring in an independent bookkeeper once a month. That bookkeeper could handle all the detailed data entry, freeing up your time for other projects. You'd still have the ultimate responsibility for reviewing and understanding the final numbers, but you would be excused from the time-consuming process of having to come up with them.

Payroll

Payroll—even though software makes it easier than ever before—is another repetitive but critical job that many small business owners farm out. Many bookkeepers and accounting firms offer this service, and numerous dedicated payroll service providers are also available. Most companies that offer payroll preparation services can do everything from preparing paychecks for direct deposit (or writing actual paychecks for employees who prefer that) to filing all the necessary payroll tax returns. All you'll have to do is provide signatures and money, and then record the grand totals in your books (or have your bookkeeper do it).

Taxes

Speaking of taxes, having a business opens up the gate for a lot of different tax returns. In addition to payroll taxes, there are income taxes (both for your company and for you) and sales taxes. Some businesses (such as gas stations) are subject to specialized taxes, and have to file extra returns. Accounting professionals can help you figure out which returns are required for your business, prepare them for you, and provide you with detailed filing instructions so you don't miss any deadlines.

Looking Toward the Future

When you decide to take the huge leap and start your own business, you probably aren't planning to fold it in a month or two. No one goes into business planning to fail. But without planning, success is a lot harder to achieve. That planning applies not only to getting the business started but also to keeping it going and growing.

Here's where an experienced accountant can provide invaluable help. He can help you build on any success you have achieved so far; help you turn around a business that's struggling now but has a lot of potential for success; and help you figure out the best ways to grow your company, and what you need to have in place before that expansion begins. The latter includes obtaining adequate financing, which is crucial to success. Your accountant can help you figure out how much cash you really need to get things going, as well as the best source of funds.

Chapter 2

Who's Who in Accounting

The world of accounting is populated with lots of players, but the stereotypical number crunchers no longer exist. Math "nerds" hunched over adding machines spewing yard-long tapes full of numbers are yesterday's accountants. Today, computers do all of that number crunching, leaving accountants free to get creative. You'll find accountants analyzing data, creating financial forecasts, sniffing out fraud, and even determining Academy Award winners.

The categories for accounting are broad, such as management accounting, as well as specialized categories, such as forensic accounting and internal auditing. Each of those different types fits somewhere into the three main categories: public, private, and government. In addition, there are different levels in accounting. But regardless of their level or category, accountants all primarily focus on numbers.

In this chapter you'll learn all you need to know about the different types of accounting professionals, what they do, how they do it, and how to decide which type of professional is right for you.

CPAS ARE LICENSED

Licensed to Bill

With the rise of publicly held corporations, more intricate economic dealings, and complicated tax laws, accountants find themselves in great demand. Because so many people depend financially on public corporations—for their livelihoods and their retirement accounts— there's a lot of work for public accountants to do.

Certified public accountants (CPAs) provide the highest level of services to the public, due in part to their additional education, experience, and testing requirements. CPAs jump through a lot of hoops to earn and maintain state certification, including comprehensive continuing education that ensures they will always be informed of the most current information and issues.

CPAs by the Numbers

According to NASBA (the National Association of State Boards of Accountancy), there are 664,532 actively licensed CPAs in the United States. That doesn't even include those licensed in states that don't provide data to NASBA (Delaware, Hawaii, Wisconsin, and Utah).

The journey to becoming a CPA starts in college. At a minimum, prospective CPA candidates must complete at least 150 hours of education, including a bachelor's degree. While some states allow candidates to sit for the exam before they've achieved 150 credit hours, they cannot earn their licenses until that minimum education requirement has been met. Candidates are not required to obtain master's degrees, but many do while fulfilling that 150-hour mandate.

In addition, most states have specific breakdowns of the credits that must be earned. For example, Kansas asks for 30 semester hours in accounting along with 42 semester hours in business and general education courses. Maryland requires at least 27 semester hours of accounting, a minimum of 21 hours of related subject matter, and at least three hours of ethics education. The requirements in Texas are even more stringent and include:

- At least 30 hours of upper-level accounting courses, which must include at least 15 hours of traditional in-person class time
- Two hours of accounting or tax research
- At least 24 hours of upper-level related business courses, including three hours of business communications
- Three hours of board-approved ethics courses

You can see how demanding the course work is, but it's almost a cakewalk compared to the much-feared, hard-to-pass CPA exam. And even after the education requirements are met, and the exam has been passed (followed by intense celebration), that's still not enough to score a CPA license. Every state has minimum experience requirements, meaning candidates actually have to work in accounting (usually for at least two years) before they can earn that certification.

THE CPA EXAM

Any CPA will tell you that the CPA exam is an exhausting, exhaustive, and anxiety-provoking professional licensing exam. The

American Institute of Certified Public Accountants, AICPA (discussed in detail in the following section), creates this days-long, multipart, computer-based test to make sure only the most qualified candidates earn the coveted CPA designation.

Over the years, the exam has changed quite a bit: For example, though every exam from the first in 1917 through 2003 was taken with pen and paper, now the exam is fully computerized. And the changes keep coming. In 2017, the exam was expanded from a 14-hour test to a 16-hour test, and included more "task-based simulations," though it still covers four core sections. These four exam sections are:

1. **Auditing and Attestation**, which covers topics like ethics, professional responsibility, risk assessment, and reporting on the reliability of financial statements
2. **Financial Accounting and Reporting**, which includes financial reporting, financial statement accounts, and specific select transactions
3. **Regulation**, which asks questions about federal tax procedures, business law, and federal taxation of individuals and entities
4. **Business Environment and Concepts**, which delves into corporate governance, economic concepts, financial management, and information systems

One of the biggest changes in the 2017 version of the exam involved "higher order skills," such as analysis and evaluation of information, along with more "task-based simulations." Those simulations were designed to make sure newly licensed CPAs know how to perform the tasks most likely to be assigned to them when they first start out in the field.

In order to pass the CPA exam, applicants have to pass all four parts with a score of 75 or higher within 18 months (this window may vary slightly based on state licensing laws) of the first section they pass. It sounds straightforward, but it's not. That score isn't a simple 75 percent correct; rather, a whole host of weighted factors go into determining the score for each part. Typically, scores are released two to three weeks after the exam is held. Potential CPAs may retake any parts they didn't pass as many times as necessary.

YEARLY CONTINUING PROFESSIONAL EDUCATION

One of the primary ways CPAs stay on top of the always-evolving tax laws, compliance regulations, and technical innovations is through continuing professional education. Though state law governs the specific requirements, all CPAs must complete at least some course work every year, covering topics relevant to their practices.

This continuing professional education, or CPE, covers a wide variety of issues, from professional ethics to estate planning to audit skills. Some states allow concentrated education in one subject area, others call for a variety of topics; and virtually all states require CPAs to take an ethics course in every licensing period. Alaska, for example, requires 80 hours of CPE every two years, including four hours of ethics training, with at least 20 hours completed every year. Illinois CPAs must complete 120 hours of CPE every three years, including four hours of ethics training, with no more than 24 hours of "personal development" CPE (which covers topics like public speaking and people management skills). Georgia calls for 80 hours of CPE every two years, including at least 20 hours each year; that 80 hours must include 16 credit hours in accounting and auditing education.

CPE credits come in a few different forms. In-person seminars can run for hours or days, and can be held in exotic locations (even on cruise ships). These CPA get-togethers can feature lively debates and discussions of the topics that impact the profession, the business world, and the economy. Real-time webinars offer almost the same interaction as in-person CPE, as participants can ask questions and get involved in the discussion. They also help save travel time and costs for busy CPAs trying to squeeze in CPE. CPAs can also self-study, and this form of education largely takes place online. While some self-study CPE companies still offer workbooks and fill-in-the-bubble tests, more post their lessons, materials, and tests on the Internet.

Every time a CPA renews her license, she has to attest that her required CPE hours are complete. Because ethics is such a big part of the profession, CPE reporting generally follows the honor system. But in the spirit of "trust, but verify," many states audit the CPE credits of randomly selected CPAs and require them to supply proof of their continuing education.

THE AICPA

Protecting the Public Interest

The American Institute of Certified Public Accountants (AICPA) sets the standards for professional training, conduct, and ethics for the CPA profession, and it's done so for more than 100 years. With nearly 420,000 members from 143 countries around the world, the U.S.-based association has become a global force in the accounting industry.

When the organization was created by a handful of gentlemen in New York in 1887, it was called the American Association of Public Accountants (AAPA). Over the years, the name changed, along with the membership rules. Today, the AICPA welcomes CPAs and non-certified accounting professionals alike, representing members in every practice area, from public practice to private consulting.

In addition to strict professional guidelines, the AICPA sets auditing standards for a variety of U.S. entities, including:

- Private companies
- All levels of government
- Nonprofit organizations

This makes sure that audits adhere to specific rules, and meet very high quality standards. Auditing standards include guidance on issues such as an auditor's responsibilities, auditor independence, and the form and content of an auditor's report on financial statements. Along with setting those auditing standards, the organization coordinates with FASB, offering support and guidance for setting and interpreting accounting rules. It also acts as an advocate for the profession in front of legislative bodies (like Congress) and other business-oriented entities. One of the AICPA's most important roles, though, is tracking and enforcing compliance with ethical and professional standards.

Need an Accountant?

One public service the AICPA provides is helping people and companies find the right kind of accounting professional. Whether you need a licensed Personal Financial Specialist (PFS), a CPA with business valuation credentials, or one of the other seasoned professionals accredited by the AICPA, the organization's website (www.aicpa.org) can get you started.

SETTING A VERY HIGH BAR

The AICPA sets very high standards for its members (and for all accounting and accounting-related professionals, really), particularly when it comes to ethics. They have a very strict code of conduct governing those ethics, as well as professional responsibilities.

Independence

Independence is one of the primary guiding principles for CPAs in public practice. Here, independence means that the CPA has no financial, personal, professional, or other connection to the company for which he's providing audit-type services including reviews, which offer *limited* assurance that there are no material misstatements in financial statements, a lower level of confidence than audits. This complete separation is crucial for a CPA's credibility. For example, a CPA must assure the investing public that a corporation's financial statements paint a clear picture of the company's actual financial position. Independence is vital because investors *must* be able to rely on that opinion. CPAs who violate this rule lose membership in the AICPA, and professional sanctions can include revocation of CPA status.

Integrity and Duty of Care

In addition, CPAs are expected to always act with integrity, honesty, and objectivity. They carry the responsibility of acting in the public interest at all times, and the public must be able to trust them completely. At the same time, CPAs have a duty of care requiring a high level of competence and diligence.

To uphold that duty of care, CPAs are held to very strict education standards, designed to ensure that they really know what they're doing. To test that knowledge, the AICPA creates and grades the grueling Uniform CPA Examination, which hopeful professionals must pass in full before they can merit an official CPA license. As mentioned previously, once they are licensed, the learning continues, as CPAs are required to complete minimum hours of continuing professional education in order to keep their licenses.

ADD-ON CREDENTIALS CALL FOR EXPANDED TRAINING

For CPAs who want to dive deeper into a specific practice area, the AICPA offers specialized credentials for a variety of professional niches, including:

- Personal financial planning
- Business valuation
- Forensic accounting

- Information and technology
- Management accounting

One of the most popular of those credentials is the PFS (Personal Financial Specialists) designation. PFS holders offer in-depth tax, retirement, risk management, investment, and estate planning services. To score the PFS credential, these CPAs (who must be AICPA members in good standing) bank on their extensive education and minimum five-year experience to pass a comprehensive exam that fully tests their financial planning chops. That, along with 3,000 hours of experience over the preceding five years, will make an ambitious CPA eligible to be a certified PFS.

Other designations carry similarly comprehensive requirements. For example, the CITP (Certified Information Technology Professional) title, which requires a keen ability to build a bridge between technology and business, also calls for a grueling exam and proven depth of knowledge. CPAs seeking the coveted CFF (Certified in Financial Forensics) credential must demonstrate superior skills in such areas as fraud prevention and detection, litigation support, bankruptcy and insolvency, and electronic data analysis.

Bottom line: when you hire one of these accredited professionals, you can be confident that he has the skills, knowledge, and experience required to get the job done right.

RAISING YOUR FINANCIAL IQ

A big part of the AICPA's mission involves the general public: helping people better understand and manage their personal finances. To that end, the association takes part in a lot of community outreach efforts, and offers tools and programs to anyone who wants to learn more about money, budgeting, financial planning, and taxes.

Feed the Pig

The group also promotes the Feed the Pig program (www.feedthepig .org). This program encourages young working adults to start saving money, pay down debt, and grow their wealth. By offering free tips, financial calculators, and financial planning templates online, this program outlines specific actions people can take to meet their financial goals.

360 Degrees of Financial Literacy

Another AICPA free public service is the 360 Degrees of Financial Literacy project (www.360financialliteracy.org), a whole-life Internet-based program that begins with inspiring kids to pick up good financial habits, and follows through with advice for people in every stage of life. The site offers targeted help for students, small business owners, parents, military families, and more, because every financial situation is different. A big part of the AICPA's commitment is the Financial Literacy Resource Center, which connects CPAs with volunteer opportunities and provides the resources they need to help their communities, whether they're teaching kids in elementary school about money basics or organizing community meetings on retirement planning.

Total Tax Insights

The AICPA's Total Tax Insights calculator, another free tool, is designed to help Americans get a better picture of all of the taxes they pay, including income and property taxes. The resource includes a side-by-side location comparison, so users can see how their overall taxes stack up against other places in the country. The calculator, found at www.totaltaxinsights.org, can also be used to help users make tax-based decisions and figure out estimated tax liabilities.

BOOKKEEPING VERSUS ACCOUNTING

A Financial Showdown

Bookkeeping and accounting are related in the same way that recipes are related to ingredients. Ingredients are the raw materials you need to create a meal, and bookkeeping provides the raw materials you need to develop useful financial reports. A recipe takes that pile of ingredients and tells you how to transform it into that tasty meal, and accounting helps you create reports so that you can analyze them to help you make your business or your personal financial plan successful.

Accounting Needs Bookkeeping

You cannot have accounting without bookkeeping; bookkeeping is a crucial part of the whole process. You can, however, have bookkeeping without accounting. Just as you can eat carrots and celery without making soup, you can do bookkeeping without performing any full-blown accounting tasks.

In theory, there's a wide gap between bookkeepers and accountants, but in reality the lines are often blurry. By definition, a bookkeeper compiles and records information. An accountant takes that information to the next level by analyzing that information, and then presenting it in a more useful format (such as specialized reports), explaining what all the numbers mean, and making recommendations for future action.

THE INS AND OUTS OF
BOOKKEEPING

Bookkeeping is really just what it sounds like: keeping the books. That includes every facet of recordkeeping. A basic example would be writing a check, recording it, marking it off when it has been cashed, and making sure it was cashed for the right amount. In fact, every time money is involved—even if it has not yet changed hands—there is something to record. Sometimes there is something to record even when no money at all is involved, such as when two companies trade services instead of paying each other.

Bookkeeping used to be the most labor-intensive and time-consuming part of accounting. But then computers came along and took over these bookkeeping tasks. Even so, bookkeeping is still one of the most important parts of accounting, because without it there would be no way to keep track of your business finances, let alone see how well your company is really doing. Many new or small business owners let bookkeeping slide (at least initially), because even automated bookkeeping takes up a lot of very precious time. Other business owners don't keep up with their bookkeeping simply because they just don't like working with numbers. Then, at the end of the year, they transfer their files (or, believe it or not, haul stacks of paper reports and receipts) over to the tax preparer, and wait to be told how the business is doing. The answer often is "not good." Of course, by then it can be too late for the owner to do anything about it.

Keeping your books thorough and current will help you avoid that scene, and it may also save you a lot of money at the end of the year. Yes, bookkeeping takes time, and you probably do not have tons of time to spare, but you can get around that by using easily navigated business bookkeeping software or apps, or by hiring a part-time bookkeeper. At least in the very beginning when your business is first starting up, though, it's good to do some of it on your own. This work allows you to get a good feel for how your business finances work and develop a better understanding of how everything fits together financially.

For individuals who are not business owners, bookkeeping involves tasks like recording deposits, paying bills, tracking income on investments, and monitoring cash. Just like with business bookkeeping, most of these tasks can be automatically taken care of through online banking and budget apps. But it still takes a person to make sure that everything that should have been taken care of has been.

They're Not All Accountants

A lot of people work under the accounting umbrella, but they are not all accountants—even though people think of them that way. Included in this general industry are professionals such as bookkeepers, tax preparers, auditors, and even financial planners. And while all of these professionals use accounting information to do their jobs, they don't have to be accountants. Then there are the vast number of professionals who work in accounting departments, many of whom are not technically accountants. This cadre of workers can include people like accounts receivable clerks, payroll administrators, and inventory analysts. People in these roles work with accounting information but are not required to be accountants.

By starting with the small, clear steps of bookkeeping, you will be able to more easily make the giant leaps of financial analysis and forecasting. It's like starting out in the mailroom and working your way up to the president's office: As you work your way up, you learn the ins and outs of everything, giving you a better ability to understand virtually every facet of the company.

ACCOUNTING TIES IT ALL TOGETHER

Now that you know what bookkeeping is, it's time to turn our attention to accounting. Accounting covers a lot of ground and includes everything from the framework that supports all of the bookkeeping tasks to the final analysis of what all the numbers mean and what to do with them. The science of accounting sets the rules for figuring out which events will be recorded by the bookkeepers, dictates exactly how and when that information will be set down, and most important, communicates all of this in a useful way to the people who need to know it.

That communication is both simple and complex. It includes standard reports, called financial statements, that everyone from business owners to bank managers can read. Accounting also provides the tools for analyzing those numbers—not just how they all add up, but what they mean, and how they can be used to make decisions going forward.

So, whether you want to grow your business, your retirement savings, or your personal wealth, accounting information lights the path that guides you to those goals. Without it, you couldn't chart progress, recover from losses, or measure your success. Accounting provides the context for every number in your entire financial life.

ENTERTAINMENT ACCOUNTANTS

Summing Up Show Biz

Think accounting can't be glamorous? Think again! Entertainment accountants work in the heart of show biz, right alongside Hollywood stars, Broadway producers, TV network executives, and movie moguls. Along with the glamor and glitz, these financial professionals score unique perks like travel to breathtaking location shoots, tickets to the hottest premieres, and production company swag bags.

Working in the entertainment industry requires a specific skill set, as the accounting tasks performed here don't really make sense in other types of businesses. For example, some entertainment accountants need to know the ins and outs of production accounting, whether they're working for a movie producer, a television network, or a Web-based series. Some entertainment accountants work on contracts, requiring familiarity with profit participation, syndication, and royalty rules. Others work directly for the stars, overseeing every aspect of their personal finances, from contract negotiations to estate planning to managing cash flow. And a very special few get to work on the biggest showbiz event of all—the Oscars.

AND THE OSCAR GOES TO . . .

Every year at the Academy Awards, along with dozens of Hollywood's brightest stars, two people dressed to the nines will step out of separate chauffeur-driven cars and onto the red carpet that paves the way into the awards ceremony. Though the pair will blend in with the glitterati surrounding them, they will be the only ones carrying the top-secret briefcases packed with envelopes containing the names of the year's winners.

One of the most exciting dream jobs in the accounting world goes to the handful of CPAs who get to tally up the votes for the Academy Awards, a process that starts in mid-January. This is tougher than it sounds, because the round that determines the nominees is based on some pretty intricate—and secret—math. Once those nominees are named, the accountants get a break, but it doesn't last long. When the votes for the winners are in, it's time for the next step: counting the ballots to determine a winner. And these CPAs have a very limited time to physically count thousands of votes, and then count them again, in a secret location. Each of the assisting accountants will see only a small portion of the votes, so no one will know who the winners are except for the two CPAs designated to be the vote carriers.

Those two must memorize each of the winners, because in order to avoid security breaches the results are not written down or typed into a computer. This pair of CPAs will continually test each other to make sure they both remember all of the names accurately. In the hours leading right up to the ceremony, they'll go through preprinted category cards, selecting only the victors, and stuff those cards into the ceremonial envelopes. Each accountant will take one complete set of winners in a briefcase, then head separately to the ceremony. Once there, they head backstage and prepare to hand over the envelopes to the stars presenting the awards.

But the Oscars isn't the only place you'll find entertainment accountants . . .

ACCOUNTANT TO THE STARS

Along with personal trainers, personal assistants, and personal chefs, many show biz professionals also keep personal accountants on the payroll. From actors to script writers to musicians, all of these artists have special accounting needs that are unique to their industry.

Because a lot of celebrities get their first jobs when they're relatively young, they often have no experience managing money, paying bills, or planning for the future. These celebrities need expert and trustworthy financial advisors on their teams, and they often lean heavily on their personal accountants for these services. These accountants get involved in every area that touches finances, like international currency exchange computations, managing the celebrity's cash flow, and complex contract negotiations. Those contracts might include things like royalty payments and residuals, which can be paid out over many years and so require constant tracking. For musicians and authors who go on tours, the accountant prepares travel budgets and manages the travel expenses. These artist-specific tasks are completed along with standard accountant-fare, such as annual tax return preparation and retirement planning.

What Are Residuals?

Residuals, in the entertainment industry, are payments made to performers for showings of their work after the original debut. They're most commonly talked about in the context of TV reruns, where an actor may get paid for a specified number of years (or forever) every time their show appears on TV.

SNEAK PREVIEWS FOR PRODUCTION ACCOUNTANTS

As the name implies, production accountants are responsible for the financial aspects of all sorts of creative productions:

- Movies
- Plays
- Sitcoms
- Reality shows
- And more

Since these creative productions require a ton of planning at the beginning and a lot of wrap-up work at the end, production accountants are often the first ones working on the project and the last ones to finish up. Along with the very technical requirements of this gig, production accountants must be able to work with demanding producers and competing egos in very high-stress situations. They must also be familiar with guild rules, union reporting, profit participation figures, and set insurance.

Each job that a production accountant takes on starts with securing financing and setting the budget for the project, with input from the producers or the studio. This boring-sounding budgeting task takes on a tinge of glamour when you add entertainment into the picture. How many big-name stars can the production afford? How many of the production crew will need to travel to Thailand for location shoots? Production accountants may also be intimately involved in scheduling, especially if the project requires a lot of people to travel to multiple locations without going over budget.

Once the initial budget is set, some traditional financial tracking comes in. Like other businesses, creative productions have standard expenses such as payroll, utilities, and office supplies that are mixed in with more unusual items such as period costumes, wigs and hairpieces, Lamborghinis, explosives, and set design props, among others. The production accountant is also responsible for monitoring the project's assets and liabilities, and making sure that purchases don't bust the budget.

After the production is wrapped, and the actors and crew have left for new gigs, the production accountant begins his post-production work. This may include tasks such as setting up residual payments for the actors and navigating through the complex tax laws that address the entertainment field.

Big Money in Movies

The average salary for production accountants runs approximately $45,000 a year. An experienced production accountant can make upward of $2,000 a week, if they're lucky enough to score a job on a big Hollywood blockbuster.

FORENSIC ACCOUNTANTS

If You Hide It, They Will Come

Financial fraud happens more often than you might expect. Armed with analytical minds, financial insights, and keen eyes for dodgy details, forensic accountants swoop in to uncover the fraud and take down the perpetrators. Corporate fraud, embezzlement schemes, and identity theft cases occur with alarming frequency, and it takes specialized detection skills to find the crimes and track down the criminals.

In addition to their aptitude for uncovering financial fraud, forensic accountants help law enforcement in many more ways. For example, they often testify as expert witnesses in class action lawsuits and other financially leaning trials. They help settle contract disputes and insurance claims. These forensic accountants also work hard to prevent financial crimes from ever taking place by helping corporations and public institutions beef up their computer and Internet security, and by putting fraud-detecting procedures in place. Even with all of those protections in place, financial fraud occurs daily, keeping forensic accountants in constant demand.

License to Probe

The AICPA offers a specialized certification for CPAs skilled in fraud detection. With special education, training, and experience, intrepid accountants can qualify to be CFFs (Certified in Financial Forensics), and then work to take down scam artists, hackers, and pirates.

THE BILLION-DOLLAR DECEPTION

Every year, trillions of business dollars are lost to fraud. That's why the demand for forensic accountants is at an all-time high: These are the guys who detect the money trail and follow it with their keenly honed analytical skills. Tracing the money and tracking down these high-level criminals takes a lot of determination, intuition, and a knack for noticing the smallest details. Among the crimes that these financial detectives solve are:

- Fraudulent insurance claims
- Embezzlement
- Telemarketing swindles
- Bankruptcy fraud
- Misappropriated assets
- Financial statement scams

And while the biggest frauds—like the Enron scandal or the Bernie Madoff scheme—get all the attention, virtually every business is at risk. In fact, according to the *2016 Global Fraud Study* put out by the Association of Certified Fraud Examiners, an average organization loses about 5 percent of revenues to fraud every year. That translates to upward of $3 trillion lost to fraud worldwide. The report also highlights the most common type of fraud (asset misappropriation, where insiders steal from the company, like embezzlement), and the least common type (financial statement fraud, where corporations report purposely misleading information on their statements). And although financial statement fraud occurs in only about 10 percent of financial fraud cases, the median loss caused by financial statement fraud hovers around $975,000.

JOINING THE G-MEN

Back in 1908 the FBI was first formed, and that first rush of agents (sometimes called G-men) included a lot of accountants. In fact, accountants comprised more than a third of those original agents, and they truly pulled their weight. It was the accountants who brought down famed mobster Al Capone, arresting him for tax evasion even as he neatly dodged other criminal charges.

Combat Training for CPAs?

Unlike Ben Affleck's character in the movie *The Accountant*, hand-to-hand combat skills aren't required for forensic CPAs. And while these professionals are proficient with numbers, most can't compute complex equations using just a glass wall and a dry-erase marker . . . or analyze more than a decade of accounting data in under a day.

It's not easy to join the G-men as a forensic accountant. To even apply, hopeful accountants must have completed either a bachelor's degree with at least 24 semester hours of accounting or a master's degree in accounting. On top of that, the agency prefers applicants to have at least one professional designation, including CPA, CFE (Certified Fraud Examiner), or CIA (Certified Internal Auditor). Once an accountant is accepted into this limited-membership club, she'll be tasked to aid the Bureau in ongoing investigations, working cases involved in counterintelligence, cybercrime, organized crime, and more.

DIVORCE ACCOUNTANTS

Forensic accountants don't track only criminals. These days, their uniquely honed skills are often used to dig up hidden funds in divorce cases. Sadly, these niche professionals are in demand, and that demand is rising.

Too often, one spouse will try to hide or understate their earnings, their ability to earn, or their personal assets (like retirement benefits or separately owned properties) in an effort to minimize alimony or child support, or to skew the division of property. In cases like these, the unsuspecting spouse can only fare better with a forensic accountant on the team. This professional can bring uncovered information to the negotiating table, ensuring that the proceedings will be fair to both parties.

But while many divorce accountants specialize in hunting for concealed assets, others help uninformed spouses (where the other spouse has exclusively handled all of the couple's money) understand the financial situation. Also, in cases with complex finances, one or more businesses, or a significant amount of assets, a forensic divorce accountant can help untangle thorny issues for the couple.

To do this job well, the accountant has to be comfortable with handholding, as the people who hire "divorce accountants" are often in raw emotional states. Spouses with no financial experience can be terrified of the prospect of having to manage all the money on their own, and worry about not having enough—especially when there are children involved.

These professionals don't come cheap, often charging between $200 and $300 per hour for complex divorce cases. Having one on your side, though, can be well worth the cost, especially if it turns out that your soon-to-be-former spouse does have assets hidden away.

ANTI–MONEY LAUNDERING SPECIALISTS

Sniffing Out Dirty Dollars

Money from illegal enterprises fuels terrorist and criminal organizations around the world. Literally trillions of dollars of illegal trade takes place every year, and the kingpins have gotten very adept at concealing their money trails. While you may think that their biggest financial challenge is bringing in more cash, what actually causes them problems is transforming the dirty money from illegal activities into squeaky clean, perfectly legal funds. That process is called money laundering, and tracking that cash has opened up a whole new branch of accounting for people called Certified Anti–Money Laundering Specialists (CAMS).

IT'S A DIRTY JOB

Anti–money laundering specialists are tasked with a nearly impossible mission. Chasing down laundered money has gotten increasingly difficult as more criminals use the Internet to cover up their illicit activities. Online banking and payment services, mobile phone money transfers, and virtual funds (like bitcoins) make it harder than ever to uncover illegal transactions.

But even though it's difficult, these specialists are committed to completing their task. Tracking these illegal funds and cutting them off at the source helps stop the world's worst crimes and most dangerous terrorist organizations. It's no wonder these specialists earn top annual salaries, which average somewhere around the $100,000 mark.

Many of these dedicated professionals work right where the money is, at financial institutions. There, they oversee the systems, making sure strict protocols are followed and ensuring that all systems comply with regulatory requirements. They also monitor transactions closely, always on the lookout for suspicious activity.

FOLLOWING A DIRTY DOLLAR

To track down the criminals and find the cash, anti-money laundering specialists need super skills and intensive training. They have to be highly proficient in forensic accounting, thoroughly understand the intricate facets of risk management, and be adept at statistical data mining. But tracking laundered money takes more than highly honed financial detection skills. It also requires dedication, determination, patience, and imagination. But actually laundering money doesn't require quite as much brainpower. In fact, once a successful laundering operation is set up, the money practically washes itself.

Flush with ill-gotten gains, a money launderer washes his money through three basic stages:

1. Placement—moving money into the legitimate financial system
2. Layering—breaking up dirty money into small amounts and shuffling it around to obscure its path
3. Integration—getting the money back from "clean" sources

Money launderers commonly create or use cash-based businesses (such as vending machines or laundromats) to scrub their illegal funds (like in the television series *Breaking Bad*, where they used car washes to clean the money from meth sales). The criminal business owner simply adds some dirty cash to the company's legitimate daily receipts, and then deposits the money all together in the business bank account for later distribution back to the owner. In other cases, they may buy portable and hard-to-track commodities (like diamonds), and sell them in another jurisdiction to clean their cash. Online auctions and gambling sites are also used frequently to launder money.

BACKTRACKING: FROM CLEAN BACK TO DIRTY

Despite the many laws and regulations that have been put in place, money launderers continue to find new ways to clean their dirty funds. Starting back in the 1970s when governments instituted the Bank Secrecy Act, which required documentation when clients had "suspicious looking" transactions of $10,000 or more, criminals simply began making increased smaller transactions to get around the rules. And as smart as anti–money laundering specialists are, the criminals tend to run steps ahead, finding new creative ways to make their dirty money disappear, which in turn makes the specialists' tasks increasingly difficult.

The trail always starts with a transaction or detail that strikes the specialist as suspicious. He may be tipped off to the transaction by an informant, or notice that a person's means doesn't match his lifestyle. Once he begins to follow that thread, the anti–money laundering specialist collects clues to build a case. Every transaction leads to another, and soon the tapestry carefully woven by the money launderer is unraveled by the anti–money laundering specialist. It's a painstaking, time-consuming quest that culminates in catching the bad guys and in a very satisfying career.

Deposits by Smurfs

Smurfs are money launderers who move small, undetectable amounts of dirty money. They may carry it in suitcases across international borders, or make dozens of deposits across a region.

CFOS STEER CORPORATIONS

Fat Cats Get All the Gravy

CEOs (or Chief Executive Officers) get all the glory. But it's the CFOs, the Chief Financial Officers, who keep the corporate wheels turning. These are the money guys, the ones who set the big-picture financial strategies for companies, from R & D (research and development) budgets to tax planning to IPOs (initial public offerings).

CFOs generally report directly to the company's CEO, providing him with the financial data that forms the foundation for decision-making. In addition, the CFO of a public corporation usually presents such information directly to the company's board of directors. He also deals directly with taxing and regulatory agencies like the SEC (Securities and Exchange Commission).

CFOs Strike It Rich

The median salary for a CFO in the United States is an incredible $310,823 per year (as of October 2016). That's before bonuses, benefits, and perks—which can bring the total compensation package closer to $500,000.

SHOW ME THE MONEY

Before CFO titles were all the rage, controllers (the professionals in charge of a company's finances) handled the financial affairs of a business. Their duties were more limited than those of a typical CFO, but those duties still fall to the CFO to handle. Controller's tasks mainly look to the past, focused on reporting on and analyzing what the company has already done, as opposed to future planning.

The CFO's controllership duties still include responsibilities like preparing and presenting accurate and timely financial statements to the upper management team of the company. In public corporations, this information would also be given to the board of directors, corporate shareholders, employees, and creditors, as well as to financial analysts and brokers outside the company.

Crucial decisions are made based on the information provided by the CFO, such as:

- Expansion plans
- Downsizing and layoffs
- Acquisitions and mergers
- Stock offerings
- Debt financing
- Major asset purchases

With a strong, forward-thinking CFO advising the CEO and the board of directors, profitability can be maximized, layoffs and cutbacks minimized, and successful expansion realized.

KEEPING THE DOORS OPEN

While informing everyone about the company's financial condition takes up a good deal of the CFO's time, his most important duty is keeping those finances above water. This part of the job was once done by someone holding the title of "treasurer," but it now falls into the CFO's domain.

At the most basic level, these treasury duties call on the CFO to manage the company's money, making him the key responsibility holder when it comes to its current financial condition. Whether the money is rolling in or hemorrhaging out, the CFO must develop high-level strategies to deal with the flow of funds. Among those duties, the CFO must:

- Determine where to invest the company's funds
- Ensure the company has enough liquidity to meet current obligations
- Figure out the most advantageous combination of debt and equity financing
- Engage in financial planning and analysis to ensure future cash flows

Without a keen sense of how money flows in and out of the company, and a high-level understanding of the industry and the overall economy, a CFO could run the business into the ground. That's why only the most insightful, experienced financial accountants are able to do this demanding job well.

LOOK INTO MY CRYSTAL BALL

To compete in a vast and always changing environment, companies must focus on the future. The CFO moves his company forward by employing financial forecasting strategies. To do that successfully, the CFO must have clear insights into the company's strengths, and create focused plans on how to capitalize on that information. For example, the CFO of an appliance manufacturer has to know which models are bringing in the most money, and which have the strongest sales potential moving forward. In addition, he must have the ability to determine how to use that knowledge to boost future sales and spur corporate growth. For example, he could shift more funds into production and advertising for those top-selling models to increase customer purchases, and (as a result) company revenues.

To accomplish these goals, the CFO creates financial models to evaluate different scenarios, and then predicts which will be most advantageous for the company. The success of the company hinges on how accurate those models are, and how well the CFO is able to anticipate upcoming economic events. If the CFO of that appliance manufacturer does his job well, the company will see soaring sales and a larger customer base. If not, the company might end up overstocked with products it can't sell. Which way things pan out can make all the difference to a company's success, and determine whether the CFO will keep his job.

TAX ACCOUNTANTS

A Taxing Profession

Most people only think about their income taxes in March or April. Tax accountants think about them all year round, and that pays off for you in a big way. These savvy professionals keep up-to-the-minute tabs on frequently changing tax laws and scour the tax code looking for ways to help their clients get bigger refunds. They also home in on each client's unique situation to help them keep more of their income now and in the future.

And while popular tax prep mills give their representatives at least some basic training, that training is usually focused more on using the company's proprietary software than in understanding the tax laws and utilizing money-saving strategies for clients. These enterprises emphasize volume, trying to churn out as many tax returns as possible, instead of paying attention to high-quality personalized service.

A seasoned tax accountant, particularly a CPA, will cost more than do-it-yourself software or tax preparation chain stores. However, if your financial picture is more complex than a W-2 and a standard deduction, it may be well worth the expense to hire a qualified professional tax accountant who can find you even bigger tax savings for the current year and beyond. The bottom line is, you really get what you pay for.

TAX AVOIDANCE: THE AMERICAN WAY

Here's the golden rule of taxes: Tax *evasion* is illegal; tax *avoidance* is the American way. While tax avoidance sounds illegal, it's not.

What it really means is figuring out the absolute minimum taxes you owe legally using existing laws, deductions, and loopholes. That's why, despite the fact that the market is full of do-it-yourself tax software, people still go to accountants to get their annual income taxes prepared and filed.

CPAs know that the best way to slash your tax bill is to reduce your taxable income as far down as it will go. That can slide you into a more favorable tax bracket, where your income is taxed at a lower percentage. Other completely legal strategies may involve:

- Taking advantage of every available tax credit
- Maximizing tax-free income
- Shifting income
- Maximizing deductions
- Deferring taxes

Your tax accountant will identify which of these strategies you can use to minimize your income tax bill. Some are incredibly simple to employ, others can be tricky, and truly call for professional guidance. As long as there's no fraud, theft, or deception involved, you're well within your rights to avoid paying even a penny more in taxes than you have to.

TAX IDENTITY THEFT ON THE RISE

Millions of Americans have fallen prey to tax identity theft, and agency insiders worry that the numbers may get worse. This crime has caused widespread systemic problems over the past several years, and it takes a terrible toll on the victims. During the 2016 tax season, nearly 60 percent of CPAs surveyed had at least one client who had fallen victim to this fraud, according to the *Journal of Accountancy*. Many of these clients had no idea that the theft had occurred until they went to file their returns.

Here's how the scam works: A criminal gets hold of some basic personal information, including a social security number. Then they go to the IRS website to get a copy of the individual's tax return from the previous year. This gives them a wealth of additional information. The thief then uses that information to create and file a fake tax return, directing the refund to himself. When the real taxpayer goes to file his return, it's rejected because a refund has already been issued to that social security number. As you can imagine, it's very difficult to resolve this problem and get the refund that's really owed to you.

This Is Not the IRS

The IRS doesn't contact people by text, email, or social media to inform them about tax issues. The agency also doesn't demand payment over the phone. If someone claiming to be from the IRS contacts you in any of those ways, don't buy it. It's a scam.

How can a tax accountant help set things straight? First, and most important, an accountant will help you navigate through the tax system and negotiate with the IRS to make sure you aren't subject to any fines or penalties related to the theft; after all, it is illegal to file a fraudulent tax return. He'll also work with the IRS to resolve the issue, and file all the related forms (such as Form 14039, which reports the identity theft), so you can file your legitimate return and get your refund as soon as possible.

AUDIT HELP

Should you have the misfortune of being called in to the IRS for an audit, your tax accountant—as long as he's a CPA—will be there to represent you, right by your side, taking charge of the meeting. (Certain other tax preparers who have special credentials from the IRS may also be able to represent taxpayers whose returns they've prepared, but only in a limited fashion.)

Much fewer returns are audited than most people realize, and the IRS tends to select returns they expect to generate additional taxes. If your return is selected, and you get a letter from the IRS, don't panic. Many times, issues with your tax return can be resolved with some paperwork, and won't involve a visit to the local IRS field office. Contrary to TV dramas, audits rarely end in criminal proceedings or bankruptcy; they almost always involve simple mistakes or questionable deductions.

If you do get called in, you have options for how to represent yourself. You can go it alone, bring your CPA with you, or your CPA can appear without you (saving you the stress of coming face to face with the IRS auditor). Armed with the correct information, such as documentation for the deduction in question, the matter can be resolved quickly. However you decide to handle the situation, *do not ignore it.* If you get a call or letter (by postal mail, never email) from the IRS, you must respond within 30 days; every day of nonresponse after that tacks on interest charges.

RED FLAGS: WATCH OUT FOR UNSCRUPULOUS PREPARERS

As software has made basic tax return completion easier, virtually anyone can hang out a shingle as a professional tax preparer. That does not mean, however, that they know what they're doing, or that they've had any training at all. These preparers may be willing to take more and riskier deductions or fudge income numbers to score you a higher refund, especially if their fee is a percentage of how much you're getting back. That in itself is a red flag; reputable professionals do not base their fees on the refund amount.

Other red flags to watch out for include:

- The preparer refuses to sign the tax return
- The preparer doesn't have a valid PTIN (Preparer Tax Identification Number)
- You're asked to sign a blank or incomplete return
- The preparer recommends direct-depositing the refund into an account that's not yours
- The preparer doesn't e-file your return
- The preparer asks to see your last paystub rather than your W-2

These unscrupulous tax preparers can pocket your refund, steal or sell your identity, or ruin your credit. If you do choose to have your taxes done professionally, make sure to find someone reputable, like a CPA.

ENVIRONMENTAL ACCOUNTANTS

It's Not Easy Being Green

Sometimes the cost of doing business includes damage to the environment, an issue that's increasingly taking center stage. As concern grows and regulations get more complex, environmental accountants step in to weigh those costs against profits, reputations, and future business. In the best cases, environmental accountants can help save the planet while increasing company profits.

Traditionally, cleanup costs, compliance fittings, and allowances for fines or penalties were lumped in with general overhead costs, and were considered an overall cost of doing business. That way, the costs were never directly associated with a process or a product. Environmental accounting specifically changes that, clearly identifying environmental costs and tracing them directly back to their source. With that detailed information, management can make better decisions about reducing or mitigating damage to the environment.

The $62 Billion Cleanup

The Deepwater Horizon oil spill—then the largest spill in American history—splashed across headlines in April 2010. The BP rig exploded in the Gulf of Mexico, killing eleven workers and releasing millions of barrels of oil into the water. In October 2015, BP agreed to pay more than $20 billion in settlement claims, bringing the total cleanup price tag to nearly $62 billion.

While some industries, such as oil production and transport, very obviously need these niche professionals, their expertise is also called on by businesses you might not expect. The clothing industry, for example, uses a lot of hazardous chemicals when creating their fashions, from the pesticides used in cotton farming to the toxic dyes that color our clothes. Growing sugarcane also costs the environment dearly through habitat destruction, water-poisoning fertilizers, and substantial industrial waste. Those are just a few of the ways industries can impact our environment and environmental concerns can affect a company's bottom line.

WHAT EXACTLY IS AN ENVIRONMENTAL COST?

When you think about environmental costs, you may picture a duck covered in oil, or a polar bear floating on a lone ice floe. In the accounting world, though, these costs center on business and money in the form of lost profits, bad publicity, government fines, and expensive cleanups.

Specific environmental cost considerations (in the accounting sense) include things like:

- Evaluating alternative chemicals, as one may cost more initially but cause less damage down the line
- Finding different disposal methods for toxic substances to prevent exorbitant cleanup costs
- Considering alternative power sources (such as solar or wind) to cut down on air pollution

Now, more and more companies are working to avoid or minimize any environmental damage, especially if it helps boost their bottom lines. An environmental accountant is particularly handy to have on staff to help make such determinations.

COMPLIANCE LAWS

In addition to traditional accounting skills like math prowess and attention to detail, environmental accountants must also have a thorough understanding of very complex compliance laws and very technical scientific material. They use accepted accounting principles to figure out the costs of environmental disasters and cleanup (like when an oil pipeline bursts), as well as model and predict potential future issues.

Many industries have begun to hire environmental accountants to minimize their costs and maximize profits. The standard corporate duties these professionals carry out include things like:

- Calculate the cost of environmentally friendly alternatives
- Help companies create cleaner profitable products
- Help companies use their resources more efficiently
- Trade environmental credits
- Identify ways to monetize waste products
- Take advantage of special tax advantages and credits

While many environmental accountants work for private industry, some hold government jobs (with the EPA—Environmental Protection Agency—for example) or work for nonprofit organizations. In a government role, the accountant may be responsible for tasks like tracking natural resources or calculating how much prevention initiatives will cost.

CHOOSING THE RIGHT PROFESSIONAL

Are You the One for Me?

Once you decide you want to turn to an accountant for help, your next step is to figure out what level of help you're looking for and what specialty areas you need. Doing that will point you toward the right kind of professional. You may use a mix of professionals. For example, you might hire a bookkeeper to handle the day-to-day data entry for your business and have a tax professional to do your business and personal income tax returns at year-end; or you may decide to do all of the basic bookkeeping tasks in-house, but hire out the payroll processing. Taking an honest look at what you can do, what you want to do, and what you probably won't do (at least not regularly) will help you decide whom you need to hire.

Many new and small businesses forge close relationships with their accountants, and consult with them frequently right from the startup stage on through to expansion. In such a case, you may think of your accountant as a paid partner in the business, which means that the personal side of the relationship can be as important as the professional side. The most important elements of this relationship are confidence and trust: You must feel confident that your accountant knows what she's talking about, that you are getting sound advice, and that you can trust your accountant with a lot of highly confidential information.

What else should you do before choosing an accounting professional?

CHECKING THE CREDENTIALS

Before you hire a CPA, especially if you just picked him out of the phone book, you should verify his license to practice. You can check the status of any CPA's license with the appropriate state licensing board. If his credentials are not in good standing, cross off that name and look for someone else. CPA licenses can be suspended or revoked for dozens of reasons. For example, simply failing to renew a license on time, neglecting to update contact information, or not keeping up with annual CPE (continuing professional education) requirements can result in license revocation or suspension.

CPAverify.org

A quick way to verify a CPA license without struggling to find the right page on a tough-to-maneuver government website, is to visit the CPAverify.org website (www.cpaverify.org). If you know the accountant's first and last name, you can find all the states he's licensed in with a single click.

On the much more serious side, CPAs can also lose their licenses for ethics violations, criminal activity, misconduct while conducting an audit, failing to return clients' documents, and client contract violations, such as not performing work he was hired to do. In addition to revoking and suspending licenses, other punishments and penalties may apply in these instances, such as fines and formal reprimands.

THE MONEY FACTOR

When you're looking to hire an accountant, cost is definitely something to keep in mind. As you would expect, higher-level services such as tax planning cost more than lower-level services such as bookkeeping data entry. Higher-level professionals may offer lower-level services, but there's a pretty good chance that they will charge more than the going rate, even if they do charge less than their standard rate. If you need soup-to-nuts help, consider a full-service firm with different levels of employees for which the firm bills different rates. That way you can get bookkeeping rates from your CPA firm for that level of service, even though you pay higher fees for the higher-end services.

More Letters, Higher Fees

In most cases, CPAs charge more for their services than do any other professionals in the accounting industry. The more letters attached to their names, such as CIA (Capital Investment Advisor), the higher the fees climb. In exchange for those higher fees, though, you get the benefit of their extensive experience and unique insights.

Prices vary widely across the country, but you should be able to find prices for business services within some basic ranges (or at least very close). Straight bookkeeping generally costs between $30 and $60 per hour. For bookkeeping services on a monthly contract basis, you can expect to pay between $200 and $600 per month, depending on the volume of transactions.

Payroll services (which all small businesses should absolutely consider using) typically charge their fees based on the number of employees you have, along with how much of the process you expect them to perform. An average small business with four employees that uses an online payroll firm (like SurePayroll, OnPay, or Gusto), which does everything from preparing the paychecks (which includes employees paid by direct deposit) to making the tax deposits to filing all the year-end paperwork, can expect to pay somewhere around $40 to $60 per month (plus the cost of actual payroll and taxes).

CPAs and accountants charge relatively high hourly fees, and some may have graduated fee structures based on specific tasks. Creating reports and similar tasks are likely to fall toward the lower end of that scale, but exactly where they fall depends on the complexity of both your business and the volume of reporting requirements. Bankruptcy services, business advice and planning, tax advice and planning, and other consulting services all fall at the high end of the scale. There can be a lot of variety here, but expect the numbers to start at about $150 to $250 per hour, ranging to $750 to $1,500 for an average business tax return. On the plus side, every dime you spend here is fully deductible on your company's income tax return.

YOUR COMFORT FACTOR MATTERS

Choosing an accountant involves more than Googling "accountants near me" and calling around for prices. The professional you choose may become intimately involved in your business and in your personal finances. You may look to her for advice about how to keep your company afloat, how to help it grow, and how to bring your kids on board. On the personal side, she could handle your taxes and tax planning, and set up college and retirement accounts.

It's important to pick someone you can trust, both to lead you and your company in the right direction and to honor the confidentiality of sensitive and sometimes personal financial information. You want to choose someone who has a lot of experience with the specific services you need, and with businesses like yours. An accountant who specializes in retail shops, for example, may not be the best choice for a physical therapy and massage group.

Equally as important as all that, though, is finding someone you genuinely like. You should feel secure asking questions about anything that could affect your company. In fact, you should feel free to be able to bring up questions about your personal financial business, especially if it is intertwined with that of the company. Your accountant should be someone you'd go out to lunch with or bring along to a ball game. At the same time, you must feel confident enough in her advice to follow it. And, of course, when you disagree with that advice, you also should feel comfortable saying so.

Chapter 3
Setting the Framework

Now that software and apps have taken over so many basic book-keeping tasks, it may seem useless to learn about tedious-sounding accounting details, like knowing the different types of accounts and how they work with each other. But if you want to see your business succeed, it's important to understand your books, from setup to annual financial statements, even if you hire an accountant or book-keeper to run the numbers for you.

Accounting isn't only about collecting payments and taking care of bills; it's also about using numbers to support your vision for the company, and help it grow profitably. In this chapter, you'll gain a clear picture of how your accounts interact, what a ledger and a journal are, how transactions get posted, and why closing accounts at the end of every period will give you a better sense of your business and its finances.

ACCOUNTING STARTS WITH ACCOUNTS

The ABCs of Accounting

As you might expect, a business accounting system is made up of accounts. Here, accounts serve as a way to group information, sort of like a financial filing system. For example, everything that happens with cash, such as writing a check or depositing the day's cash register take, gets run through a cash account. And the monthly checks to cover rent on the office all show up in both the cash and the rent expenses account.

Almost any grouping that would be meaningful to the business can become an account. Of course, there are some standard accounts, and some standard account names, such as Cash and Depreciation Expense, that you will find in almost every company's bookkeeping system. There are also plenty of specialized accounts that are unique to particular businesses and don't really apply anywhere else. For example, a florist would not need a "ketchup and mustard" account, and a hot dog vendor wouldn't need a "ribbons and bows" account. All companies, though, have the same basic account structure, and follow the traditional account conventions.

PERMANENT VERSUS TEMPORARY

Every account falls under one of two main categories:

1. Permanent
2. Temporary

Permanent accounts are the ones that show up on the balance sheet, and they include assets, liabilities, and equity accounts. These accounts stay in place from year to year, accumulating information the whole time. Temporary accounts show up on the income statement, and they include revenues, costs, and expenses. These accounts only hold on to the information of a single accounting period, however long that period may be.

At the end of every accounting period, the temporary accounts get folded into permanent accounts, as the net income from the period is added (or subtracted, in the case of a loss) into the appropriate capital account (which depends on the business structure, such as partnership or corporation). Then each temporary account gets zeroed out to start the new period with a clean slate. What's the point of this? Well, permanent account balances are measured at a particular time; for instance, the cash balance on January 12. Temporary accounts are measured for a period of time, such as racking up sales during February 2017. Those temporary accounts need to be reset so you can begin tracking them again. Meanwhile, the overall net activity of those temporary accounts needs to be permanently added to the records, and this is done by folding them into the permanent accounts.

Nothing but Net

In the world of accounting, net activity has nothing to do with fishing and everything to do with combining account balances. When you net accounts together, you combine their balances to see how much they're worth mixed together. So if account A showed $10 and account B showed -$5, then their net activity would be $5.

ACCOUNT NUMBERS
KEEP THE ORDER

There is no part of accounting that doesn't involve numbers, and the accounts themselves are no different. In addition to a descriptive name, an account number is assigned to each account. This cannot be done haphazardly because doing so would wreak havoc on your records. Believe it or not, accounting is designed to simplify how you deal with your business finances; and doing everything according to tried-and-true systems will make it all even easier.

The basic accounting convention, built into virtually every accounting software system—even if you don't see it—is as follows. Traditionally, asset account numbers start with 1, liability accounts with 2, equity accounts with 3, revenue accounts with 4, cost accounts with 5, and expense accounts with 6. Depending on how many accounts you have overall, you would add anywhere from one to ten digits to a given account. For example, if you have hundreds of asset accounts, you could use a three-digit account numbering system to track your assets, and each of those account numbers would start with 1 to follow that convention: your main cash account might be number 101, your inventory account 120, and your first fixed-asset account 150.

HOW THE ACCOUNTS CONNECT

A System of Checks and Balances

At some point, every type of account will interconnect with each of the others. Every single transaction your business conducts involves at least two accounts, sometimes more, and they most often are of different types. For example, assets will be used to pay for expenses. Inventory products bought on account involve both assets and liabilities. Product sales hit both cost and revenue accounts. Owner withdrawals deplete both assets and equity. Transactions are typically catalogued by time, based on the date they occurred; for more detail and trackability, some transactions include reference numbers like invoice or check numbers.

In addition to that, though, the accounts have to be in perfect balance, like any equation. The company's total assets must be exactly equal to its combined liabilities and equity. To get to that balance, the net result of combining the revenue, cost, and expense accounts must be folded into the equity account. That perfect balance is clearly displayed on the company's formal financial statements.

THE FORMAL CONNECTION

Periodically, you or your accountant will produce a set of financial statements for your company. These statements are formal reports that spell out exactly what has been going on for the preceding period (regardless of how long that period is), and where things stand at the time you create the statements. How often you run the statements depends on the type and size of company, the company's tax situation, and how regularly you (as the business owner) want to monitor the company's finances. Most business owners prepare financial statements at least quarterly so they can pay quarterly estimated income taxes as necessary. There are three main financial statements that you will put together. These statements are:

1. The balance sheet
2. The statement of profit and loss
3. The statement of cash flows

Basically, the balance sheet represents the "accounting equation" (assets equals liabilities plus equity). It shows that the equation is in balance by providing a snapshot of the asset, liability, and equity accounts on a particular date.

The statement of profit and loss informs you of your revenues, costs, expenses, and business results (the profit or loss, commonly called the bottom line) for a specific period of time.

Finally, the statement of cash flows shows you how the money came into and went out of your business during that same specific time period. This statement usually includes every account type, as they all have some relationship with cash.

With these three statements in hand, a business owner can see the full financial picture of his company, and see whether his efforts have resulted in profits for the period. For a more in-depth discussion of these crucial business tools, check out Chapter 6.

THE EVERYDAY CONNECTION

For many small businesses, daily transactions include three types of accounts:

1. Revenues
2. Expenses
3. Cash

These are the accounts that will be involved in the vast majority of day-to-day transactions. The company's checking account is often the first place in which these transactions are recorded. For example, collecting cash from a client for services rendered will hit both the cash and revenue accounts; while paying the store's electric bill affects both the cash account and an expense account.

More Than Two

Sometimes a transaction will impact more than two accounts. For example, if you pay for phone service, cable, and Internet all on the same bill, that transaction would affect four accounts: phone expense, cable expense, Internet expense, and cash.

When you bring products for resale into the picture, then inventory and liabilities become everyday accounts as well. Each time you purchase inventory for your business, you'll owe money to the company you bought it from—a increase to the liability account. And even though you won't necessarily see a daily entry for purchase or sales transactions in your equity accounts, they are affected by every revenue and expense transaction because at the end of the accounting period, the total net income (or loss) from that period gets folded into the equity accounts.

Connections Keep the Business Moving

At the most basic level, both everyday and formal periodic connections among the accounts are what keep your business flowing. In other words, you use a combination of liabilities and equity to purchase assets. Assets are your company's resources, and you use those assets to create revenue, some directly (like inventory that converts into a sale) and some indirectly (like the computer used to account for the inventory). It's easy to see a clear link between inventory and revenue production, but seeing how the computer can help bring in revenue isn't quite as obvious. But your computer does generate revenue when you use it to create invoices, design promotional flyers, keep your books in order, learn more about your industry, and find new ways to bring in customers.

Expenses also go directly toward revenue production. After all, you can't run a business without things like phones, electricity, Internet access, and pens. Those revenues and expenses come together in your business, hopefully with revenues greater than expenses, to create additional equity.

DEBITS AND CREDITS

The Secret Language of Accountants

One of the most basic—and most confusing (at least at first)—concepts of accounting involves debits and credits. This concept is usually one of the first things taught to accounting students, and is one of the later things that clicks, because at first glance it seems counterintuitive. The debit/credit scheme, though, lies at the heart of every accounting system. Once you have a grasp of how debits and credits work, you will understand much more easily how the whole system works.

SO WHAT *ARE* DEBITS AND CREDITS?

In the world of accounting, debit means left, and credit means right. At first glance, that might seem confusing. But in the beginning of double entry accounting (the modern system we all use now), when everything was done by hand using pencil and paper, it was the only way to go.

Every single accounting transaction has at least two parts, a debit side and a credit side, and the two have to be equal. The word "side" here is crucial. In old-fashioned, traditional manual accounting systems each individual account was set up like a T (and called a "T-account" on the paper.

Here's the tricky part. Some accounts are increased by debits; some are decreased. In the same way, some accounts are increased by credits, and others are decreased. Whether a debit or credit acts like an addition or subtraction completely depends on the type of account you are working with. Check out the following table to see which accounts work in which ways.

DEBITS AND CREDITS		
ACCOUNT TYPE	DEBIT	CREDIT
Asset	Increase	Decrease
Liability	Decrease	Increase
Equity	Decrease	Increase
Revenue	Decrease	Increase
Expense	Increase	Decrease

That's how all business transactions are recorded, based on this ages-old debit/credit accounting system. But there a few times when it seems like debits and credits are backward.

Inside a T Account

Here's how a T account works: The account name goes on top of the T, all debits to that account go on the left side of the T, and all credits on the right. Every time a transaction affected that account, the bookkeeper would record the dollar amount on the appropriate side of the T, debit or credit; and the type of account determined which side was appropriate.

THE BANKING SWITCHEROO

When it comes to personal finances, there's an extra twist that makes debits and credits seem more confusing than they really are. Think about the cards in your wallet: debit cards and credit cards. They don't match the traditional scheme because their names weren't created by accountants, but by bankers, and from their perspective.

When you use your debit card, it decreases the amount of money you have in your bank account. But it also decreases the amount of money the bank owes you. So from the bank's perspective, every time you use your debit card, it decreases their liability—and, as you saw on the table, liability accounts *decrease* with a debit.

Here's the twist: Every time you use a credit card, you're technically borrowing money from the bank. So every swipe increases the amount of money you owe the bank. From the bank's perspective, they're extending credit to you. When you pay for things with your credit card, it increases their asset (a receivables account), which *increases* with a debit.

On the bank's side, whether you use a debit card or credit card, the accounts on their books get a debit entry. But on your side, in your personal finances, every time you use either a debit or credit card, your "books" get a credit entry; you're either decreasing your cash balance with the debit card, or increasing your liabilities with your credit card.

SOMETIMES IT'S THE OPPOSITE IN BUSINESS, TOO

In business accounting, there are some accounts that act in completely the opposite direction of the other accounts in their group when it comes to debits and credits. For example, some asset accounts have normal credit balances, and some sales accounts have normal debit balances. These special accounts are called contra accounts, because they act contrary to the norm (which is how they got that nickname).

Though contra accounts may seem puzzling, they serve a very clear purpose. They can help you separate certain kinds of transactions from their "parent" account (the account they're offsetting), giving you a clearer picture of what's really going on. Sometimes that breakdown is very important, so much so that it can affect your future business strategies and policies. For example, suppose your company sells hand-knit sweaters. Most of those sales will be final, but there are bound to be some returns. If you just lumped those returns into your sales account, sort of like negative sales, you would have no way of knowing how many sweaters you sold altogether and how many sweaters were returned. Instead, you would just see one lower sales number with no breakdown.

For planning purposes, it's important to know what percentage of your sweater sales resulted in returns. An expected percentage of returns might not cause you to take action, but a much higher percentage of returns than you were anticipating probably would.

Here's an example. Your company sold thirty sweaters for $50 each, for a total of $1,500. Ten of those sweaters were later returned, dropping that total by $500. If you just took the $500 returns out of the $1,500 sales, the books would show $1,000 in net sales ($1,500 - $500). That would be technically correct, but not as informative as breaking out the two numbers.

SALES AND RETURNS ACCOUNTS		
Sweater Sales		$1,500
Less: Returns	$500	
Net Sweater Sales		$1,000

If you saw only the $1,000 net sales figure, you wouldn't know that one-third of those sweaters had been returned, only that 20 were sold. Having the full picture, using the separate contra account for returns, offers more detailed and correct information, allowing you to make better business decisions going forward.

BREAKING DOWN A TRANSACTION

Being in business creates an enormous pile of transactions (events that have some kind of monetary impact), which you'll learn more about in just a moment. Every one of those transactions has both a debit and a credit component. That does not mean that the transaction necessarily involves a plus and a minus (although that may happen sometimes), or that one account balance will go up while another goes down (which may also happen). Rather, every transaction will have a left-side impact (debit) and a right-side impact (credit). How a transaction *affects* the relevant accounts depends completely on what kind of accounts they are.

For example, suppose you write a check to pay the company's electric bill. That transaction would result in a debit to electricity expense and a credit to cash. Your electricity expense is increased, and cash decreased. If you change that transaction a little, the account impact changes, too. Suppose you paid that electric bill with a credit card; you would still debit the electricity expense, but now the credit would go to an account like "credit card payable," one of your liability accounts. In this case, the expense account increases, and so does the liability account (because now you owe more).

During the next month, you pay the company's credit card bill. That transaction includes a debit to the credit card payable account and a credit to cash. Credit card payable, the liability account, gets decreased with a debit (the payment reduced your balance). The cash account, an asset, is decreased as well, but this type of account gets decreased with a credit entry.

WHAT COUNTS AS A TRANSACTION

Did Money Change Hands?

A business transaction takes place when an event that can be measured in terms of money has occurred. That's the formal definition, and it takes a bit of unpacking. There are dozens, probably hundreds, of events that happen in every business on any given day that have no monetary effect at all: opening the mail, Skyping with clients, and sending emails, for example. Turning those occurrences into transactions takes only one thing, and that is money. If that envelope you opened held a check from a customer, you have a transaction to record. If that Skype call resulted in a sale, you'd have another transaction. If those emails contain promotional links for customers to click on and buy products, each email-based sale would count as a transaction.

Most companies have the same general transactions, and those get repeated all the time. Common transactions include:

- Making sales
- Collecting money
- Paying bills
- Paying employees
- Paying taxes
- Purchasing supplies
- Receiving inventory
- Buying equipment

Every transaction causes changes to occur in specific accounts, changing what you owe or what you own. When you record a transaction, you have to know which accounts are affected, and how; when the transaction took place; and the dollar value of the transaction (even if no money has changed hands yet). Sometimes, though, knowing when to record the transaction isn't as straightforward as it seems.

WHEN TO RECORD TRANSACTIONS

In accounting, as in most other things, timing is everything. Timing applies to transactions themselves, in two different ways:

- The first involves the day the transaction actually took place (for example, you buy a case of copy paper and some toner, and have the office supply store bill your company).
- The second comes into play when money changes hands (you send out a check for those office supplies).

These two things may happen at the same time (for instance, if you paid for the supplies while you were still in the store), but just as often they won't. The trick is knowing when it's time to record the transaction, and that depends on the accounting method you decide to use for your business.

You have two distinct options to choose from for your overall accounting method:

1. **The cash method**, more commonly used by very small businesses and small service businesses, means you only record transactions when money changes hands. Using this method, you wouldn't record that paper and toner purchase in your books until the day you actually paid the office supply company.

2. **The accrual method**, which many companies have to use, requires that you record transactions as they occur, regardless of the money factor. Under this method, you would write up the transaction on the day you got the office supplies, then use a second transaction to record the payment.

Let's take a closer look.

Cash Accounting

When it comes to choosing an accounting method, especially for a very small business, cash wins hands down over accrual. Why? Because:

- It's easier to understand: You record transactions when cash changes hands.
- It gives you a little leeway at year-end to minimize taxable income: You can pay a bunch of expenses early to reduce your profits and your tax bill for the year, and you only pay taxes on the cash you have actually received that year.
- The actual bookkeeping is much simpler: Since all transactions involve cash, you only need to worry about the other accounts involved in the entry.

There is a very big drawback to this much-preferred method, though: timing. The cash method doesn't track your revenues and expenses as they happen in real time—only when there's a payment involved. Knowing exactly when the original transactions occurred could come in very handy for planning purposes, because you would know in which actual accounting period the expense was incurred or revenue earned. For example, if you sold holiday decorations in

December, but didn't get paid until February, that sale would be recorded in February, a completely different accounting period.

On top of that, some companies are not allowed to use the cash accounting method, according to IRS regulations. According to the IRS, if your company has inventory, you can't use cash accounting. You also can't, under IRS guidelines, use this method if your company is formed as a C corporation (also called a regular corporation) or if your gross revenues are more than $5 million a year (a very good problem to have). If you aren't sure whether or not your company can use the cash method, check with a tax accountant.

Cash In, Cash Out

When you use cash accounting, virtually your entire bookkeeping system can be run through your checking account. As long as every check and every deposit are recorded, you will have most of your daily accounting chores taken care of. Typically, the only extra recording comes in when you pay cash for some expenses.

Accrual Accounting

Using the accrual accounting method is a little bit more complicated than the cash method, but it can provide you with better and timelier information. Traditionally, keeping the books in this way required active double entry accounting, meaning you always had to specify which two accounts (or more, when applicable) were affected by each transaction. This differs from the cash method, because in that case, it is assumed that no matter which account the transaction was posted to, the other one is always the cash account. With software now automatically recording transactions in the proper accounts, this drawback no longer really affects bookkeeping to the same extent. But it's still a little more complicated to do than cash accounting, and a little trickier to understand.

The basic rule of accrual accounting is to record transactions as they happen, even if no cash is involved at the time. You record every sale (revenue) as it is earned and every expense as it is incurred. The underlying accounting principle here is called the matching principle. That is, you match revenues and expenses to the period in which they actually took place.

When you buy supplies on account, you record the transaction on the day you bought the supplies. When you make a sale to a client, you record the sale that day, even if your invoice doesn't ask him to pay you for another 30 days. Of course, when the cash does eventually change hands, you will have another transaction to record. Having to record those extra entries is one of the drawbacks of accrual accounting. The other drawback has a bigger impact on your bank account, namely you have to pay income taxes on revenues you have earned, even if you have not yet been paid.

Timing Is Everything

With the accrual method, the noncash entries are the ones that impact your bottom line. Their purpose is to record revenues and expenses right now. When you do pay those expenses or receive those customer checks, those transactions have no effect on your profits, since the transactions involve only assets and liabilities.

THE ACCOUNTING CYCLE

Report. Rinse. Repeat.

Traditionally, an accounting cycle refers to the processes and procedures performed to record a company's transactions. The cycle starts with a transaction, moves through the creation of financial statements, and ends with a closeout. There are, of course, a number of other steps in between. Why is it a cycle? Because after the last step is completed, the whole process begins again.

Though a lot of the steps are now invisible thanks to accounting software, it's important to know what the steps are and what actually happens even if software is doing all the work. The complete traditional accounting cycle can be summed up in eight basic steps. Accountants:

1. Record transactions in the daily journals
2. Post journal entries to the appropriate ledgers
3. Prepare a trial balance of all general ledger accounts
4. Create a working trial balance, complete with adjusting entries
5. Enter those adjusting entries into the general journal, and then post them to the general ledger
6. Prepare a set of financial statements
7. Close out the temporary accounts
8. Create a post-closing trial balance

Knowing the steps, and what order to take them in, is essential to the accounting process. Taking those steps, and getting into the meat of the numbers, is when the work really begins.

TAKING THE STEPS

You probably record transactions, which is the first step in the accounting cycle, every day. When you break it down, this step involves recognizing what counts as a transaction, identifying all the details pertinent to that transaction, and then recording those details in a journal. A journal is a sort of transaction diary (more on that in a moment). Before the use of accounting software became widespread, those journal entries would be periodically posted to ledgers, which are books containing pages for each specific account. This is step two. So if a journal entry included the cash account, eventually that part of the transaction would be posted to the cash account's ledger page (sort of like a check register). With accounting software, this happens automatically, as soon as the journal entry gets recorded.

Divisible by 9

Because it was so hard to find mistakes in handwritten journals and ledgers, bookkeepers developed little tricks to track errors. For example, if the trial balance was off by an amount that was cleanly divisible by 9, then the bookkeeper knew there was a transposition error—a reversing of the digits in a number, like 19 instead of 91.

Step three, the trial balance (which we discuss in more detail later on in this section), is a way to make sure everything has been posted correctly. As the name of this step suggests, it's basically a test to see if the accounts balance. To create this report, you list all the accounts in the ledger along with their ending debit or credit balances; then you add up all the debits and all the credits. If the total debits equal the total credits, the accounts balance; if not, there's a mistake somewhere. In the presoftware days, bookkeepers would pull their hair out trying to find the mistakes that knocked the trial balance out of whack. Now, software does this automatically, and it virtually never allows the accounts to be out of balance (though in certain circumstances, such as improper account setup, out-of-balance trial balances may occur).

Step four—working trial balance—brings adjustments into play. Sometimes, those adjustments simply correct errors. Other times, they account for things that haven't been recorded yet because of timing. For example, if the accounting period ends on a Tuesday, but your company pays its employees on Friday, you'd have to adjust the payroll expenses to capture two days' worth of employee pay (for Monday and Tuesday) in the period that's ended. Finally, adjusting entries in this fourth step are used to account for periodic depreciation and amortization expense (depreciation marks the decline in value of physical assets over time; amortization reflects the portion of an intangible asset—like a patent—that's been used up). These adjustments were traditionally recorded in a working trial balance (one that the bookkeeper would write all over—a work in progress) until everything was correctly accounted for and in balance.

Step five simply formalizes the adjusting entries made in the working trial balance. In this fifth step those entries get recorded in the journal, and then are posted to each relevant account in the ledger (another invisible step when using software).

Step six is one of the most important for business owners: creating a set of financial statements. (We'll take a closer look at those statements in Chapter 6.) The three primary financial statements are:

1. The balance sheet
2. The statement of profit and loss
3. The statement of cash flows

Together, these financial statements sum up all of the activity for the period, and offer a detailed picture of the company's current state.

Steps seven and eight wrap up the accounting cycle. First, all temporary accounts (revenues, costs, and expenses) get zeroed out, and their net total gets folded into an equity account called retained earnings. This is done to accurately capture the activity of the accounting period. Once all the closing entries have been recorded and posted, step eight comes into play: The post-closing trial balance is created to ensure all the accounts are still in balance. (This trial balance is created after the closing entries are complete.)

After that end-of-period wrap-up, there's a clean accounting slate to go forward, into the next period. Then the accounting cycle begins all over again.

JOURNALS AND LEDGERS

Journals and ledgers are throwbacks to when bookkeeping was done by hand, and each served a unique purpose:

- **Journals** were used to record transactions as they happened.
- **Ledgers** were used to carry the balance of each account.

Before computers, these physical books could get unwieldy, especially for larger organizations and inventory-based companies. That gave rise to special journals and ledgers to make it easier for book-keepers and accountants to more quickly find specific information they needed.

Special Journals

Most companies tend to have the same transactions over and over again. For the transactions that take place more frequently, like sales, bookkeepers use one of the standard special journals (in this case, the sales journal). There are four commonly used special journals:

1. Sales
2. Purchases
3. Cash receipts
4. Cash payments (also called disbursements)

Transactions that don't occur as often get recorded in the general journal, a kind of catchall for things that don't really fit into a specific category. The general journal is also the place for adjustments and closing entries.

Special Ledgers

On top of that, there are some individual accounts that merit special ledgers. Accounts receivable and accounts payable both hold summary information for a lot of underlying accounts. Accounts receivable includes everything your customers owe you, and accounts payable includes everything you owe to your suppliers. Chances are, though, that your company has a lot of different customers and uses at least a few different vendors. For each, you have to track the individual account balance so you know at a glance which customers owe how much money, and how much you owe to each supplier. That gets extremely cumbersome if it is all squished into the general ledger accounts.

For that reason, both accounts receivable and accounts payable have special subledgers. Where the general ledger holds detail information for each separate account, the subledgers hold the detail data for each customer and vendor account. Rather than posting specific transaction information to the general ledger, transactions involving accounts payable and accounts receivable first get posted to the special subledgers. Then, a summary entry is made to the general ledger accounts.

Accounting software does use these special journals and ledgers, but all of the transaction recording is done instantly and simultaneously. For example, your accounting software maintains a customer ledger so you can track payments from each customer.

A TRIAL BALANCE TALE

Though it may seem obsolete, thanks to accounting software, the trial balance provides a valuable business tool. Yes, everything should automatically be in balance—because software won't let you enter unbalanced transactions—but just because a transaction is balanced, it doesn't necessarily mean it's correct. For example, a $50.00 sale could be accidentally entered as $5,000; the entry would be balanced, but wrong. A quick look at the trial balance might let you see that something is off (for example, if the monthly sales usually hover around $2,000, but this month they're clocked in closer to $7,000).

And there are times when things don't balance, even when you are using software. For example, switching from accrual-based to cash-based reports can cause a glitch in your trial balance. Further, different software programs may have different quirks that leave the accounts unbalanced. Whatever the cause of the error, the trial balance is where you can track down the problem.

On top of that, a trial balance is the very first thing your accounting software will ask for: It needs to start someplace, after all. Whether you're just launching a new business or moving your books from one software program to another, you'll need to fill in the account balances.

Will a New Company Have Account Balances?

Yes, even a brand-new business has some balances to enter: startup costs, cash, and equity, at the very least. Most also have at least some assets (computers, office furniture, inventory) and some debts to account for.

A MATTER OF TIMING

An accounting cycle marks the beginning and end of an accounting period, but the length of that period is up to you, based on what makes sense for your business. The most commonly used timeframes are months, quarters (three-month periods), and years. Publicly traded companies are legally required to file reports at specific times, so their cycles typically follow those rules.

An accounting period is also known as a fiscal period. These periods often step in sync with the calendar, but they don't have to. For example, it could make sense for your company to end its fiscal year on June 30 (maybe you prefer to take the summer off).

Once you've set the time period to define your accounting cycle, you have to remain consistent. After all, consistency and organization are two of the main cornerstones of accounting.

ACCOUNTING AND ORGANIZATION

Order from the Chaos

Organization is the secret key to accounting—imagine what things would look like if the numbers just floated around haphazardly. You'd never know which customers owed you money, for example, or why you were writing checks. Systematically sorting revenues and expenses, customers and vendors, lets you focus your energy on growing and tending your business. If your records are chaotic, your company's chance of success plummets. You need to know where the numbers stand in order to figure out where they might go.

The act of recording transactions, along with other bookkeeping tasks, adds structure to your business. That kind of organization is also crucial to your personal financial life. Here, we'll take a look at the most efficient ways to systematically organize your and your company's finances, starting with managing every piece of paper.

THERE'S STILL A LOT OF PAPER

By now you have probably noticed that accounting involves dozens of forms, hundreds of other pieces of paper, and thousands upon thousands of numbers. Keeping track of all that information can be tricky, though accounting software makes it a lot easier. Having a system in place that tells you how and when to fill out every form, what information you need from each piece of paper, and where all of those numbers go makes the whole thing manageable. The hardest part can be putting the system in place!

Physical Organization

You should use clearly labeled file folders to keep your accounting data organized. Even if your bookkeeping takes place in the cloud, there's most likely still a paper trail for many of your transactions, and you need an efficient way to track those papers. Optimally, businesses keep one set of files for their vendors, another for customers, and a third for general expenses. In addition, it's important to set up a file for each asset and liability that shows up in your books. For example, keeping separate folders for each different vendor, rather than just shoving them all in the same file, helps you more easily track down purchase orders and invoices in the event of a problem or disagreement. Finally, and very important, all businesses should maintain files for paper copies of all tax returns, including sales tax and payroll taxes. Making sure there's a specific spot earmarked for each piece of paper (and there will still be a lot of them) will make your job much easier down the line.

Shorten Your Stack of Papers

Sick of receipt stacks? Start scanning them, or snapping photos of them with your smartphone. The IRS accepts electronic versions of receipts, as long as they're organized and clearly show the business purpose. Like paper, keep these e-receipts for at least six years.

Accounting Procedures

The physical organization of your paper is just one piece of the puzzle, though. You also need to come up with procedures for your accounting tasks. Having a single standard way of doing things will streamline your tasks, and will make it much easier when you turn over the job to someone else. Daily transactions can pile up quickly if you don't enter them as they occur. Plus, you can't produce even rough financial statements if your general ledger (the book that holds the details for every account) isn't up to date. Developing a routine is pretty much the only way to get a handle on this considerable work; without one, the bookkeeping can get away from you before you know it.

GET YOUR PERSONAL DUCKS IN A ROW

Keeping accounting information organized isn't just good for business—it can make your personal financial life easier, too. When your finances are organized, you won't accidentally skip paying a bill or depositing a check. Receipts you need for your taxes won't end up in the recycling bin. You'll have instant access to your bank balances, investment accounts, and retirement plans, all without having to search through piles of papers looking for the account numbers.

Even though organization is very important at tax time, good organization can help your finances stay on track year round. Developing a budget is one of the best ways to get organized and stick to a system. There are some great personal budgeting apps out there (like Mint .com, www.mint.com; or Mvelopes, www.mvelopes.com) that can help you stick to your plan and keep track of all of your expenses.

TRACKING TAX INFO

Whether for business or your personal life, you already know that you need records and receipts to do your taxes. It's especially important to keep track of expenses and deductions in case IRS auditors come calling. The best way to avoid future problems is to carefully organize the paperwork as you get it.

When you shell out for a deductible expense, jot down the business reason right on the receipt immediately, so you don't forget. If you prefer physical receipts, keep storage folders or envelopes everywhere you collect them (in your car, your desk, your briefcase, your gym bag). If you prefer higher-tech solutions, scan your receipts as soon as you get them. Either way, collect all the information and tally it up regularly—it's easier to do that once a month rather than face an enormous pile once a year.

If you're a DIY type, spreadsheets offer a simple way to organize and sum your expenses. If those expenses relate to your personal taxes, you can stop right there. If they're for your business, enter them into your accounting software so they can be seamlessly integrated into your company's financial records.

Some online services can also help both small business owners and personal taxpayers keep their information organized. Shoeboxed (www.shoeboxed.com), for example, lets you send in a stack of receipts (either in paper form, photos, or scanned) that is then organized into a personal online database for you, taking some of the stress out of tax time.

WHAT TO KEEP, WHAT TO TOSS

Accounting clearly creates a lot of records, and it's tough to know which things you need to hold on to (and for how long) and what you can discard. For example, you'd hold on to a purchase order at least until the vendor delivered exactly what you wanted, and sent an invoice, so you could make sure you got what you ordered and the vendor billed you correctly. If you had a sales agreement with a client, you would keep that until all the terms of the contract were fulfilled, and your company had been paid in full. The reason for keeping a document, and the amount of time you'd keep it, depends on what type of document it is. While there are no "written in stone" rules except for government requirements, here are some good basic guidelines (including some important IRS rules) to follow:

- Keep all of your tax records and external tax documents—like W-2s, 1099s, and 1098s—for at least three years after the return was actually filed
- Hold on to receipts for deductible expenses of $75 or more
- Create a long-term storage system (at least seven years) for crucial documents like employee records, bank statements, contracts, and payroll and payroll tax records
- Keep paid medical bills, paid tuition bills, charitable contribution receipts, and business/personal mileage logs for at least five years
- Hang on to your income tax returns for at least seven years

Conflicts arise all the time in the accounting world, for both business and personal reasons. Anyone (or any company) can be the subject of an IRS audit, or be involved in a contract dispute. Having the right paperwork on hand can make all the difference in your case.

For more comprehensive lists of all the business and personal documents you should keep based on your unique situation, you should talk to your accountant or financial advisor.

Chapter 4
Assets, Liabilities, and Equity

One of the foundations of accounting is the accounting equation:

assets = liabilities + equity

The three pieces of that equation can define both your business and your personal finances. They tell you what you have, what you owe, and how much of what's yours you truly own. You could not manage your personal financial situation or run your company without them. On the personal side, these three factors determine your income needs, your credit rating, and your overall wealth. The three pieces are equally crucial for your business, because they are the tools you use to generate revenue.

In this chapter, you'll learn everything you need to know about assets, liability, and equity and how they fit together in both the accounting equation and your financial planning.

THE ACCOUNTING EQUATION

Stick to the Formula

This equation, assets = liabilities + equity, sits at the very core of accounting, expressing one of the most central accounting basics: everything must remain in balance. Changes in one side of the equation require changes in the other.

The form of this equation comes from the basic idea that assets are financed with a combination of liabilities and equity. You can pay for your company's assets by using existing capital, by raising additional capital, or by borrowing funds. The transactions will be different, but the accounting equation will remain in balance no matter which way you go. For example, when you use existing capital to finance an asset purchase, you are spending resources you already have. That transaction results in a debit to the new asset, and a credit to whichever asset you used to buy it (such as cash or a traded-in vehicle). Though individual asset balances are affected, the total asset balance is not, and the equation remains in balance.

The same balance holds true when you raise new capital to purchase an asset for your company. Your asset account and your equity account will increase by equal amounts, maintaining the balance. Financing your assets with debt (like taking out a mortgage to buy an office building) acts exactly the same way: assets increase, but so do liabilities. As long as each individual transaction has equal debits and credits, your books will remain in balance, and the accounting equation will hold true.

A PERSONAL LOOK AT THE NUMBERS

In theory, the accounting equation seems pretty simple—just three factors to account for. In real life, things can get a little more complicated. But filling in numbers makes complicated situations much more clear.

What's Your Net Worth?

"Net worth" is another name for equity, and what it's usually called in the realm of personal finances. In the best circumstances, assets (what you have) exceed liabilities (what you owe), for a positive net worth. But if loans and credit card debt get out of control, or your home's appraisal value drops, a negative net worth could arise.

Let's take a look at how the accounting equation covers your personal finances. We'll use a common example: your house. As a homeowner, you own your house, or at least a big chunk of it; the part you don't exactly own yet is your outstanding mortgage. In terms of the accounting equation, it looks like this: house = mortgage + equity.

Say you bought your house for $250,000 with a $15,000 down payment and a $235,000 mortgage. Your accounting equation would look like this:

$250,000 (asset) = $235,000 (liability) + $15,000 (equity)

As you pay down your mortgage, the numbers shift, but always stay in balance. So after several years pass, your equation might look like this:

$250,000 (asset) = $223,000 (liability) + $27,000 (equity)

Your home is just one part of your total financial picture. You also probably have some bank accounts, some credit card debt, a house full of furnishings and "stuff," a car, a car loan, and a retirement fund. All of those pieces fit together like a puzzle to form a perfectly balanced accounting equation.

A REAL BUSINESS EXAMPLE

In business, it's actually much easier to see the accounting equation in action, because everything is already accounted for and categorized. To get a handle on any company's accounting equation just look at their balance sheet.

For example, Facebook released its annual balance sheet on December 31, 2015. This report indicated that the company had total assets of $49,407,000. Facebook also reported total liabilities of $5,189,000, and total shareholders' equity of $44,218,000. So, putting it all together, Facebook's accounting equation on that date was:

$$\$49,407,000 = \$5,189,000 + \$44,218,000$$

Every single transaction that has occurred since then has altered Facebook's accounting equation—and that includes the many companies they've acquired, beefing up their assets and their global reach.

WHAT ARE ASSETS?

Make Your Assets Work for You

So while you know now that assets are a crucial component of the accounting equation, here we're going to take a deeper dive into the world of assets, and their accounting impact. Equally (and maybe even more) important, we'll talk about how specific assets can be used to grow net worth.

On the business side of things, assets are those things that your company owns, from the computer on your desk to the file cabinet in the backroom to the delivery van in the driveway. It works the same way for your personal assets. The money in your checking account, your clothes, your 60-inch flat screen TV, and the fork you just used at dinner all count as assets. It does not matter whether your assets are big or small. All that matters is that you or your company owns them, and that they have monetary value. For that matter, assets don't even have to be physical things. Patents and copyrights, for example, count as assets even though you can't touch them. Also, anything you or your company has a legal right to get, such as a tax refund or a future payment from a customer, is accounted for as an asset.

Assets seem deceptively easy to understand, but the category comes with some unexpected twists—there's a lot more to learn here, as you'll find out a little later. Right now, we'll take a more general look at why assets are so important in both your personal life and in business, and how they factor into your total financial picture.

EVERY BUSINESS HAS ASSETS

No matter how small your business is, no matter what industry your company is part of, your company has assets. From a computer used to prepare customer invoices to a 20,000-square-foot processing plant, every single thing your company owns is an asset, as long as you can assign a dollar value to it.

Some assets are physical, such as chairs, copy machines, and delivery vans. Others are legally binding promises, such as accounts receivable, which is the money owed to your company by its customers. Still others seem to exist more on paper, though they may also have tangible form, such as the company checking account or prepaid expenses (for example, a year's worth of insurance paid in advance). Regardless of the form it takes, anything with monetary value that your company owns or owns the rights to (such as the right to collect money from customers who owe it) counts as an asset.

Your company's assets appear on its balance sheet, which is one of the main financial statements produced at the end of each accounting period. On this report, the assets will be split into different categories to make analysis easier. The order in which you list them on the balance sheet typically matches the way they appear in your chart of accounts (a formal listing of every account and its corresponding account number), which is usually in the order of liquidity (how quickly they can be turned into cash).

Assets do more than just show up on reports, though. They are the resources your company uses to produce revenue, and revenue is what keeps your company alive. Your business cannot bring in sales without assets, and while this connection is more clear for product-based businesses, which could not produce a dime of revenue without inventory to sell to their customers, it's true for service companies as well. At the very least, you have to have cash to pay your expenses, and to help get the word out that your company exists. Service companies also need basic tools to provide service to customers: a hair stylist needs a chair, scissors, and styling tools; an accountant needs a computer and a lot of file cabinets.

PERSONAL ASSETS

You probably don't think about this very often, but just like in a business, everything you own is your asset. And while this might not seem very important, sometimes it will be. When you apply for a loan, the lender may ask to see a personal balance sheet—and your assets will be the highlight. If you buy homeowner's or renter's insurance (which you absolutely should), the insurance company may ask for a list of your assets. So when the occasion arises, it's important to know what you have.

The big stuff is obvious: house, car, motorcycle, boat, or truck. But other personal items that count as assets may not be as apparent. When you're taking stock of your assets, make sure to include:

- All of the money in savings and checking accounts (right now)
- Investments
- Retirement accounts
- Jewelry (including watches)
- Furniture
- Appliances (refrigerator, washer/dryer, microwave)
- Electronics (phones, tablets, TVs, computers, game consoles)
- Bicycles
- Artwork

- Collectibles
- Home décor
- Fitness and sports equipment
- Tools (power tools, lawnmower, screwdriver set)
- Kitchen items (dishes, cookware, silverware)

Everything of value that you own is your asset. The items that don't quite fit into the categories listed get lumped into personal property, things like your clothes (unless they're high-end designer clothes and fur coats), sheets and towels, and kids' toys. Even if these personal items aren't individually all that valuable, all together they can add up to thousands of dollars.

When Assets Don't Count

Sometimes you use assets that you don't own, and those wouldn't count as *your* assets. For example, if you live in a furnished apartment, the furnishings do not count as your assets; neither would a company car, or a lawnmower borrowed from your neighbor—no matter how long you hold on to it.

BREAKING DOWN ASSET CATEGORIES

It's All in the Timing

Since there are so many different kinds of assets, they get split into categories to make the accounting less cumbersome. There are four commonly used groupings, which are pretty standard across businesses:

1. **Current assets:** Current assets include anything that is *expected* to be turned into cash or used up within one year, such as inventory or cash itself.
2. **Investments:** The investments category contains holdings, such as mutual funds or municipal bonds that are not really used in the normal course of business; they're a way to make some extra income using funds that the company doesn't need to use for anything else right now.
3. **Fixed assets (also called "property, plant, and equipment"):** Fixed assets have relatively long lives, and they are regularly used to support regular operations; examples include trucks, desks, and computer systems.
4. **Intangible assets:** Intangible assets are long-term assets that have no physical form but are still worth money to the company, such as a corporate logo or a trademark.

Basically anything that is expected to be converted to cash within one year of a company's balance sheet date is considered a current asset; all other assets are plunked down into one of the long-term categories (investments, fixed assets, and intangible assets).

Even within these broad categories, the assets have a particular pecking order. For example, your current assets have a liquidity pecking order. Cash is already cash, so it always comes first. An asset like prepaid expenses (such as payment of a whole year's rent in advance), on the other hand, comes with a fixed use-up date, which usually makes it the last current asset listed. Fixed assets have their own ranking system as well, but that organization is based on how long you expect the assets to last, also known as their useful lives. For example, a delivery truck might have a 10-year useful life, while an office building could last for 30 years.

Liquid Gold

Liquidity refers to how easy it would be to turn an asset into cash if you absolutely had to. Your checking account counts as cash, making it 100 percent liquid. Inventory normally moves pretty fast, and so it could be considered a quick liquid asset. By contrast, your company's customized delivery truck might take a long time to sell, and so it would not be considered a liquid asset.

CURRENT ASSETS TURN TO CASH

Current assets include anything that could be or that you expect to be converted into cash within a year of the date on your balance sheet. These assets are listed in their order of liquidity, from cash down to the current asset that you expect would take the longest to convert to cash (usually a prepaid expenses account). Here are the most common current assets, in order of liquidity:

- Cash, which includes every cash account plus any cash you have on hand
- Accounts receivable, which is money your customers owe you for sales you made to them
- Inventory, which includes anything you will resell regardless of the form it's in now
- Short-term investments, such as stocks or bonds that you plan to cash out within a year
- Prepaid expenses, which are expenses paid in advance of use, such as insurance or rent

The more current assets you have on your books, the more liquid your company is. For small businesses and startups especially, liquidity can mean the difference between success and failure.

The "Other" in "Other Income"

Long-term investments often provide current earnings, such as interest or dividends. Those earnings have to be included when you figure out your profit or loss for the period. Since they aren't regular revenues, they are reported separately, usually as "other income" at the very bottom of the statement of profit and loss.

LONG-TERM INVESTMENTS

When your company is doing well and you have extra cash lying around, you may choose to invest that money so it can earn even more. Any investments that you make and plan to hold on to for more than a year fit into the long-term investments category. These investments could include stocks, bonds, ETFs (exchange-traded funds), mutual funds, and even high-yield CDs; they also can include assets such as buildings that you are holding for investment purposes only, rather than using within your core business.

Long-term investments are often used to build asset reserves that can eventually be used to finance expansions, thereby minimizing the amount you would have to obtain from outside sources. Outside capital can be costly: bank loans always come with interest payments, and bringing on investors or business partners dilutes your ownership. Instead of taking the cash as an owner's withdrawal (or dividend), and hoping to be able to put it back in when it's needed, many small business owners instead invest that surplus cash, and then sit back and (hopefully) watch it grow.

As your expansion plans get closer, and you think the time is coming to liquidate those investments, you can shift your long-term investments into your short-term investments. Investments you expect to sell within the upcoming year transform into current assets for the company's balance sheet.

FIXED ASSETS

Any physical asset that your company owns and does not intend to sell falls into the fixed-asset category. Fixed assets range in size, useful life, and purpose. A $40 office chair counts as a fixed asset just as much as a 15,000-square-foot storage facility. The point is that they are both part of what the company needs to have in order to produce revenues, and you plan to keep them around for a long time. Fixed assets can include things such as:

- Land
- Buildings
- Building improvements
- Vehicles
- Office furniture
- Equipment
- Computer hardware

Fixed assets also come with a special contra account (an account with a normal credit balance that offsets the fixed assets account). This special contra account, called accumulated depreciation, fits in the asset category but has a normal credit balance (which is what makes it a contra account). It holds all of the depreciation expense ever taken on the connected assets. Depreciation expense tracks the declining value of assets year by year, and lets you take that decline as a tax-deductible expense spread out over the entire life of the asset. For example, if your company buys a brand-new delivery van, it starts losing value as soon as you drive it off the lot. Normal wear and tear occurs throughout the year, detracting even more from its original value. Depreciation expense puts a dollar amount on that wear and tear, to reflect the real current value of the van.

INTANGIBLE ASSETS

Some companies have assets without physical form that they plan to hold on to for the long haul. These are called intangible assets, and some companies couldn't succeed without them. In order to count an intangible as an asset, your company must own it or the rights to it, and it has to have a measurable dollar value. Some of the more common intangible assets include patents, copyrights, licensing agreements, trademarks, franchise rights, leaseholds, and goodwill (the most intangible of them all).

Goodwill can be the most confusing of these intangible assets, because it really only exists in perception, and can only be measured when a business is purchased. The goodwill asset essentially represents the reputation of a company—its good name. It only comes into accounting play when someone buys a company for more than it would be worth by the numbers alone.

Can You Put a Value on That?

It can be very hard to value intangible assets that haven't been purchased. For example, when you write a screenplay, you hold the copyright. That copyright is your intangible asset, and it's worth something, but it can be hard to determine that number. An experienced accountant can help you assign a dollar value to such assets.

Like fixed assets, intangible assets have finite useful lives over which they decline in value, at least for accounting purposes. This decline is known as amortization, and it counts as a tax-deductible expense. Since the longevity of intangible assets can be hard to pin down, their useful lives are considered to be their legal lives or 40 years, whichever is shorter. For example, a design patent issued by the U.S. government lasts for 15 years. Amortization can be held in a separate contra account, called accumulated amortization, or may simply be deducted directly from the intangible asset balance; the choice is yours (or your accountant's).

Now that we've covered the basics for each asset category, let's take a closer look at each one. The ins and outs of different asset groups may surprise you.

A CLOSER LOOK AT CURRENT ASSETS

How Quickly Can I Cash In?

As you now know, in the world of accounting the term "current assets" refers to assets that can be converted to cash within one year. These are the assets that your business would use in its everyday activities, or that you would personally use to maintain your daily finances. For making ends meet, these are hands down the most important assets you have; when you've amassed enough in current assets to get by and fund emergencies, then your focus can shift toward long-term assets and growing wealth.

In terms of personal finance, your current assets will mainly be composed of your instant cash accounts: checking and savings. While technically it would also include time-locked savings like three-, six-, or twelve-month CDs (certificates of deposit, which may pay slightly higher interest rates than "unlocked" savings), many financial advisors caution against using that money before its time, since doing so might trigger a penalty for early withdrawal that can strip away the interest you earned. Another technicality: investments (like stocks and mutual funds) count as liquid assets because they are generally easy to cash in quickly. But most people are better off not counting on these as current assets because their values can be unpredictable and because of the commissions charged when they're bought and sold.

For a small or startup business, current assets can make the difference between staying afloat and folding. If a company can't pay its bills, it won't be able to stay in business long. That's why properly managing current assets is the key to early success. Using current assets like cash, accounts receivable, inventory, short-term investments, and prepaid expenses in the most advantageous manner possible can help your fledgling business survive and thrive.

PLEASE PAY WITHIN 30 DAYS

Accounts receivable is often the largest current asset for service businesses, and among the largest for inventory-based businesses. This account describes itself perfectly: It's the amount of money you expect to receive from customers who made purchases on account. That does not include credit card sales—those count as cash. Rather, accounts receivable comes into play when your company itself extends credit to customers.

For example, if you're a freelance writer and you write an article for a client, then submit a bill to them, the amount due in that bill would be included in accounts receivable. The situation is similar for inventory-based businesses. Say your company makes custom standing desks for $500 each. A legal firm in town buys 10 desks, on account, for a total purchase of $5,000. Your company delivers the desks, and sends them an invoice. Your invoice would include the price of the desks ($5,000), plus sales tax (at 5 percent: $250), plus your $50 delivery fee. That inclusive invoice total of $5,300 ($5,000 + $250 + $50) would now be included in accounts receivable.

Managing your accounts receivable well can keep you in business; extending too much credit or letting customers slide can crush your company. No matter how much you want to make a sale, it's important to make sure your customers are going to pay you. This can be easily resolved by having your customers fill out a credit application when you first start doing business with them. That can provide valuable clues into a customer's payment history, and let you know how likely they are to pay you. In the meantime, for their first purchase, you can extend limited credit (as much as you could stomach losing) or require a large down payment.

The Trick to Getting Paid Early

Don't underestimate the power of a great deal. One of the best ways to get customers to pay quickly is to offer early bird discounts. For example, you can offer a 2 percent discount to customers that pay you within 10 days. Sure, you'll get a little less money, but you won't have to worry about collecting it.

Collections

Collections are on the other side of the deal. It's an uncomfortable chore, and a lot of small business owners simply avoid it. But if a customer has not paid you despite repeated "overdue" bill notices, you (or one of your trusted employees) will need to get tough. The first step—which will seem obvious, but a lot of companies don't put in place—is to cut off credit sales to them, and not let them buy anything else on account. If you have multiple offices or several employees, you need to make it clear to everyone that this customer's credit is frozen. The next step is contacting them in a more direct manner, whether it's by email to the company's owner or by making a call to their accounting department. Sometimes, you'll end up writing off an account. But more often than not, if you're persistent, you will get paid.

YOU HAVE TO HAVE
STUFF TO SELL STUFF

Companies that sell products need products to sell, and that means inventory. Whether you're selling ready-made goods, products that you have to assemble before selling, or products that you make, every component that goes into the items you're selling counts in inventory.

Once you have inventory, you also have to track it, and that can be tricky because (if you're lucky) this asset will move very quickly. Knowing your inventory numbers at all times is crucial to your company's success. After all, if you don't know how much you started with, how much you sold, and how much you have left on hand, how will you know when and what quantity to reorder? Having too little inventory can frustrate customers, and turn them into former customers; think of how annoyed you get when items you want are out of stock (especially if a quick web check indicated it wasn't). On the other hand, having too much inventory on hand can drag your business down when it ties up too much of the company's cash and takes up space for other items that move more quickly.

The best small business accounting software lets you easily follow inventory from the loading dock to the customer invoice. If the software you're using isn't as robust as you'd like, then you should find an inventory management app that can link with your accounting software. (A good example is SOS Inventory—www.sosinventory.com—which connects directly with QuickBooks in the cloud.) However you track your inventory electronically, you still may want to do periodic physical counts, especially if your inventory is prone to breakage (or is easy to pocket).

WHAT TO DO WITH EXTRA CASH

Once your business is off the ground, you may actually find yourself with a cash surplus. But that surplus can dissolve as quickly as it grew, due to product or service obsolescence, economic changes, or changes in your personal situation. Keeping the cash in the business can cushion your company against setbacks. Cash itself, though, doesn't work very hard these days, as savings account interest rates currently hover near zero. Many businesses therefore turn to the stock market in the hopes that they'll rack up some extra profits before they need that money back.

These short-term investments count as current assets for two key reasons. First, they're highly liquid, meaning you can sell them fast and convert them back into cash without breaking a sweat. Second, they're not part of a long-term plan, and they're not locked up in something that can't be sold quickly.

Though stocks are sometimes the preferred short-term investment, this category could include bonds, mutual funds, ETFs (exchange-traded funds), or any other investment that's easy to flip at a moment's notice.

THE SKINNY ON PREPAIDS

Prepaid expenses crop up for small and startup businesses more often than you'd think. As the name implies, this account holds the balance of expenses you pay ahead of time, and will use up later. For example, your company may pay six months rent up front for its office space. Other common prepaid expenses include insurance, legal fees, and office supplies. When a portion of the expense is actually used up, like one month's rent out of that six-month prepayment, that's when the expense gets recorded, reducing the prepaid asset account by the same amount.

Here's how it works: When your company pays the landlord $6,000 for six months rent in advance, you'd record a $6,000 increase (debit) to prepaid rent, and a $6,000 decrease (credit) to the cash account. At the end of the first month, the company will have used up one month's worth of rent, or $1,000. The entry to record that would increase (debit) the rent expense, and decrease (credit) the prepaid rent account.

THE IMPORTANCE OF CASH

Cash Really Is King

With a new or small business, cash is absolutely the most important current asset you can have. In fact, it's the *most* current asset, as cash is 100 percent liquid. Without it in plentiful supply, your business simply cannot survive. Unfortunately, many business owners confuse profits with cash, thinking that if they're earning income it means they have money. That's not always true. Learning how to effectively manage your cash flow, especially in the early, struggle-filled days, can mean the difference between success and failure for your company.

Flowing in the Wrong Direction

Product-based businesses often have money problems, at least starting out. That's because companies that sell products have to first buy them (or the materials to create them). That almost always means cash has to go out before it can possibly come in.

Even with monumental profits on the books and the promise of growing future sales, a company without cash will not make it. If you don't have enough money on hand to pay the bills, your company's vendors will stop supplying you with whatever it is your company needs to generate sales. If you can't pay your employees, they won't stick around. The number one reason why small companies go out of business is because they're out of cash. In fact, the bankruptcy courts are full of small business owners whose companies just couldn't pay the bills anymore, even though their businesses were showing profits.

Luckily, there are a lot of things you can do to prevent that dire situation. The most important one is to know how cash really flows in and out of your business. Then you can plan for shortfalls before they occur, nipping that problem in the bud. The easiest way to avoid cash crunches is to put enough money into the business at the start; absent that, you may have to contribute more capital, or take out a loan to cover temporary crises. New businesses often use more cash than they bring in during the first six months to a year, depending on the type of business. During the planning stages of your business, you would be wise to count on that happening to you, too.

PRODUCT-BASED BUSINESSES GET CASH CRUNCHED

As we discussed, in order to sell products, your company needs to have products available, and that often comes with a substantial cash outlay. New and small companies are especially vulnerable to cash flow issues, and holding products ties up a lot of cash.

The solution: Take a hard look at your inventory. It's tricky to find the right balance between having enough stock on hand and not tying up too much of your precious cash in inventory. That balance can really only be achieved with experience, but careful planning (all the way back to the planning stages of your business) can help your company start in an advantageous place. This is one of those times when an experienced small business accountant can be invaluable. She'll have worked with clients just like you and can offer helpful advice and insights on the best ways to manage your inventory flow, especially as it relates to your cash flow.

WORK WITH VENDORS

While you want your customers to pay you as quickly as possible, you also want your vendors to give you as much (reasonable) time as you need to pay their invoices. Managing your company's accounts payable, especially if you have a product-based company, can help the cash flow more smoothly.

When your business is facing a cash crunch, you can ask vendors for extended payment terms. Most of the time, they'll work with you; they want to make it easy for you to pay them. As long as you stick to a payment plan, they're likely to continue extending the credit (though it may be more limited) that your company needs to keep going.

If your company cash is in decent shape, and you can pay the bills on time, you can still stretch it to the limit to maximize cash flow. One simple way to do that is with electronic payments; even when you make them at the very last minute you will still be paying on time.

When your business is in a positive cash flow groove you can take advantage of early-payment discount terms. If a vendor offers a percentage off the invoice in exchange for early payment, and your company has enough cash on hand, take the discount. It will not only conserve cash, it also gives your company a good rep in the eyes of the vendor—and that can go a long way toward getting them to agree to extended payment terms when times are tough.

A CLOSER LOOK AT FIXED ASSETS

From Skyscrapers to Office Chairs

As we discussed, a fixed asset is anything tangible your company owns that is used (in some way) to create revenues over the long term, with a useful life of at least one year. If you can't touch it, or it will be used up within a year, it's not a fixed asset. A fixed asset also can't be something the company sells in the normal course of business. For example, if your company has a delivery van that it uses to make deliveries, it would count as a fixed asset; but if your company sells delivery vans, those would count as inventory, and not as fixed assets.

PP&E

Fixed assets include things like:

- Land
- Buildings
- Vehicles
- Heavy machinery
- Computer systems
- Office furniture

These assets are always valued at their historic cost for accounting purposes. Historic cost includes what your company paid for the asset, plus all delivery, taxes, and setup costs. Fixed assets are also often referred to as "property, plant, and equipment," or PP&E.

Land Ho!

In accounting, property refers to land and buildings. This is property you're using in the course of business, and includes things like free-standing stores, office buildings, warehouses, factories, manufacturing plants, and the land those are built on. These fixed assets are counted as yours as long as you own them or have what's known as a capital lease.

In a capital lease, your company *essentially* owns the asset, but doesn't actually own it. (Remember, this is just for accounting purposes.) In order to qualify, the lease has to meet at least one of a list of requirements, which includes that the lease period extends as long as 75 percent of the asset's useful life (for example, run at least 30 years on a 40-year building), or that your company would own the asset at the end of the lease period (sort of like renting to own).

The property category also includes major improvements and construction projects (even on property "owned" through capital leases).

Plant

"Plant" applies mainly to companies that make something, as opposed to companies that only sell finished goods. The plant category covers the kind of fixed assets you'd find, for example, in a manufacturing facility or a bakery. In this category, you would include things like:

- Manufacturing machinery
- Assembly line equipment
- Ovens and walk-in freezers
- Drill presses and lathes
- Textile machinery

Anything the company uses to create or transform goods fits under the plant umbrella.

Equipment

All the fixed assets that don't fit into the property and plant categories fall under the equipment group. This type of equipment includes things like forklifts, delivery vans, display cases, office furniture, and computer systems. These assets keep the business running, and are used in support of the business in activities like attracting customers and creating sales (as opposed to literally creating items for the business to sell).

Most small businesses' fixed assets fit into this category. Even businesses that do make products will also have this type of equipment in use. Even if your business fits into that one-man show mold (at least for now), any physical asset you're using to help bring in customers and generate sales will show up in the fixed assets section of the company balance sheet.

FIXED ASSET GUIDELINES

Fixed assets take more work than other assets, from both a real-life maintenance perspective and from the accounting viewpoint. The more substantial fixed assets, from heavy machinery to factories, can require a lot of planning (like determining the best location, getting facilities up and running, and making sure personnel have the right training) and drawn-out purchase arrangements (such as long-term leases and mortgages). Moreover, they bear the burden of being long-term liabilities to the business.

Since so much can go into fixed assets, there are a lot of guidelines to help you deal with them for accounting purposes. Some of the guidelines come from the IRS, and you may have to use them when you do your business tax return. Others come from GAAP (Generally Accepted Accounting Principles). The combined rules cover everything from what to include in the price of your asset to the method of calculating depreciation to how to record the bookkeeping entry when you eventually dispose of the asset. It sounds like a lot, but broken down, these rules are really pretty straightforward.

Calculating Fixed Asset Costs

For the more basic fixed assets, such as file cabinets, desks, and chairs, the costs are easy to determine. When you start adding in things such as down payments and trade discounts, as you would with a fleet vehicle, for instance, the accounting gets just a little trickier. The basics, though, are the same for every fixed asset you have. The accounting rule here is called the cost principle, which means that you will value your fixed assets based on what you paid for them, never based on their market value (or how much they are "really" worth). That cost, though, includes absolutely everything you had to pay to get that asset ready for work. Of course, there's the price tag of the asset itself, but you add to that things such as sales tax, delivery charges, installation, setup fees, and training on how to use the asset (common with new equipment).

Add It In

If you have to do something to your property so the asset will work properly, whatever you pay for that goes into your asset cost. For example, if a machine must be set on concrete and you have a tile floor, the cost to put in a concrete slab counts as part of your asset cost.

By the Numbers

Let's say your company needs a local computer network installed before you can get your business up and running. The system itself costs $30,000 for all the hardware and software. The installation and network management training tacks on another $6,500 to your bill. The computer company offers you a 5 percent discount on the system if you'll sign a one-year service contract for $1,500, which you do. There's 6 percent sales tax on the system and a $300 delivery charge. Before you can take delivery, though, you have to set up a climate-controlled room to house your server, and that costs $5,000. You pay a cash deposit of $500 on the room setup, another cash deposit of $3,000 on the computer system, the full price of the service contract, and the rest is payable over three years.

All of those costs—except for the service contract—go into the accounting cost of your computer system asset. That makes your asset value equal to $42,010. The system is $30,000 less a 5 percent discount, bringing it to $28,500. Sales tax (at 6 percent) on that comes to $1,710. You also add on the $6,500 setup fee, the $300 delivery charge, and the $5,000 for the climate-controlled room. Here's what the behind-the-scenes general journal entry would look like when you enter the information into your accounting software:

GENERAL JOURNAL ENTRY			
DATE	ACCOUNT PERCENT EXPLANATION	DEBIT	CREDIT
01/30/17	Computer System	42,010.00	
	Prepaid Service Contract	1,500.00	
	Cash		5,000.00
	Long-Term Loan Payable		38,510.00
Purchased computer network system with cash deposit and three-year loan, plus one-year service contract for cash.			

A WORD ABOUT DEPRECIATION

Any conversation about fixed assets would be incomplete without a nod to depreciation. Depreciation is an accounting construct designed to capture a virtual decline in value of the asset as it gets used over time. That doesn't mean the asset necessarily loses actual value—some assets don't, and some may even become more valuable over time despite ongoing wear and tear. But for accounting and tax purposes, assets get used up, and that is measured in terms of periodic depreciation expense.

The asset, or rather contra asset, account to hold all of the depreciation attached to fixed assets over time is called accumulated depreciation. Accumulated depreciation is known as a contra account because even though it fits in the asset category, where accounts are supposed to have debit balances, this account carries a credit balance. That credit balance is used to offset the value of the fixed assets.

Here's an example: Say your company has a single fixed asset that was originally worth $10,000, and you've had it for four years. Your accountant takes $1,000 in depreciation expense every year. So at the end of four years, the accumulated depreciation would be $4,000. Now, the net accounting value of your fixed asset would be $6,000, the original $10,000 cost less the $4,000 accumulated depreciation.

CURRENT LIABILITIES

Buddy, I Owe You

No matter what kind of industry they're in, virtually all businesses owe something to someone. The same holds true for most people. Whether you take out a bank loan to start a company, use a company credit card to pay for expenses, or buy your inventory from vendors on account, your company will show liabilities—debts—on the balance sheet. Even if you borrow your startup money from a family member or friend, it still counts as a liability on the company books.

Every dime your business owes, no matter to whom or for what reason, is a liability. Owing someone a product (such as a magazine subscription) or a service (such as insurance coverage) counts as a liability as well. The same holds true for your personal finances, where liabilities range from your electric bill to your credit card balances to your mortgage. All the money you owe to creditors counts as a liability.

Though there aren't as many kinds of liabilities as there are assets, liabilities also get broken out into groups, for both business and personal purposes. In your accounts you will have current liabilities and long-term liabilities. What differentiates these two types of liabilities is when you have to pay them: Anything due within one year counts as current, and any debts that stretch further out than one year go into the long-term group. In most cases, current liabilities tend to be created through daily living business activities (like purchasing inventory on account or groceries with your credit card), and long-term liabilities (which we'll discuss in more detail in the following section) and tend to be loans (including car loans and mortgages).

Most of the current liabilities your company owes will be those that come up during the normal course of business. Buying inventory on account leads to accounts payable debt, for example. Paying employees prompts payroll tax liabilities. On the other hand, most long-term liabilities (other than any startup loans) come about as the result of fixed-asset purchases or business expansions, and those are not typically everyday occurrences once your business is up and running.

"Payable" Means Liability

If you look at a business account list, you'll notice that the names of most liability accounts contain the word "payable." The rest of the name helps you see what that liability is payable for, such as "sales tax payable." The most unspecific name is accounts payable, which is a holding account for the money you owe vendors, in one lump sum.

For product-based companies, the biggest chunks of liabilities are standard fare: the business loan and the accounts payable. Service businesses such as law firms and housecleaning companies tend to have the least debt, since they usually cost less to start up and don't have to maintain stocks of inventory. Service company debts often tend to be in the form of work for which a customer has paid in advance; a good example of this would be a lawyer who works on retainer. These liabilities often have names such as "unearned revenue," and virtually always belong in the current liabilities category.

A LOT OF TAX LIABILITIES

Take a look at almost any company's current liabilities roster, and you'll find at least one—probably more—tax debts. That's because everyday transactions give rise to taxes, most of which won't be paid at the time. The most common tax liabilities a typical company would have to account for include:

- Sales tax payable, which comes into play when you sell taxable products
- Withholding tax payable, the amount of federal and state taxes you've deducted from employee paychecks
- FICA (Federal Insurance Contributions Act) payable, the "employer side" of Social Security and Medicare payroll taxes
- FUT/SUT payable, both federal and state unemployment insurance
- Property tax, any assessments on land or buildings the business owns
- Franchise tax, which some states charge based on the net worth of a company
- Gross receipts tax, another tax charged by some states, this one on a company's gross revenues

Small business owners whose companies are not set up as corporations will also have to plan for self-employment tax, which are Social Security and Medicare (a.k.a. FICA), both the amount that would have been withheld if you were an employee, plus the amount the employer would pay. This would not appear on the company's balance sheet, but would appear on a personal balance sheet (which could be required if you're applying for a business or personal loan).

MONEY ISN'T ALL YOU CAN OWE

In addition to owing money, your business can owe products or services to its customers. This liability comes about when you get paid in advance for something, and you have a legal obligation to either fulfill your part of the bargain or give the money back. Until you complete your part of the deal, whether performing services or delivering products, there will be a liability on the company books. Most of the time, unearned revenue matches up with current liabilities.

Any kind of company can have unearned revenues. Common examples include a lawyer who receives a retainer and has not yet earned the amount, a retail shop that lets customers use a layaway plan, and a contractor who gets a down payment before starting work. In each of these cases, the business gets the money up-front, before the full transaction is finalized, meaning the company still owes something to the customer and is contractually obligated to provide it.

Once you fulfill your end of the deal, the unearned revenue will transform into regular revenue. If you perform only part of the service or deliver just some of the product, only a portion of the unearned revenue will be changed into regular revenue.

LONG-TERM LIABILITIES

Forever in Your Debt

Long-term liabilities are a little more complicated than their short-term cousins. For one thing, all long-term liabilities (even personal ones) come with a current component, the part that must be paid within the next year. On the company's balance sheet, the portion of long-term liabilities that will be paid within the next year gets shifted into current liabilities. Second, unlike standard current liabilities, long-term debt comes with interest attached, and that's another liability on its own.

In your personal financial situation, you may have dealt (or be dealing) with long-term debt, usually in the form of mortgages and car loans. Those liabilities come with fixed terms (usually 30 years for mortgages, typically five years for cars), spelled-out interest rates (either fixed or adjustable), and a schedule of payments that are due periodically over the life of the loan. It works pretty much the same for businesses, deviating somewhat in the case of things like long-term capital leases and bonds (which usually only show up on the balance sheets of larger companies).

FOR YOUR SMALL BUSINESS

Like people, small businesses often take on long-term debt for mortgages and cars, but also for machinery and equipment. These are pretty standard, and they come with built-in collateral (the asset itself). But many hopeful small business owners need more, and they apply for business startup or expansion loans, in the hopes that a banker will take a chance on them. It can be very difficult to find that kind of financing, but luckily there's a way to boost your chances: the SBA, or Small Business Administration.

The SBA exists to help small businesses, and financing is one very big way they can offer guidance and assistance. With different programs for different situations, the SBA works with banks to help expand financing options for small business startups and expansions. The SBA may be able to help you even if you've already tried to get financing from the bank and didn't qualify. If you meet all of their requirements, the SBA will guarantee at least part of the loan, making it easier for nervous lenders to take the leap of faith in your company.

SBA Loan Programs Offer a Leg Up

The SBA has three basic loan programs: A 7(a) loan is the most basic, and can be used to start, buy, or expand a small business. A 504 loan provides fixed-rate financing for major fixed asset purchases. The microloan program offers loans of up to $50,000 for eligible small business borrowers. To learn more, visit www.sba.gov.

FOR INVESTORS

Big corporations have different kinds of long-term liabilities than small businesses. If you're looking to invest in a major corporation, it's important to know not only the types and amounts of these long-term liabilities but also their purposes. Along with the kinds of liabilities we've already talked about, a corporate balance sheet might include:

- **Notes Payable to Officers or Shareholders:** This comes into play when officers and shareholder-owners put money into the business without buying stock. When the notes (which are borrowing agreements, like formal IOUs) are paid back, the interest is tax-deductible to the company while dividends would not be.

- **Bonds Payable:** Sometimes corporations issue bonds (long-term debts sold to the public and used to finance things like expansions or acquisitions) to obtain financing rather than issuing more stock (which dilutes ownership). These bonds can be issued either to a specific group of investors or to the general public.
- **Capital Lease Obligations:** These are long-term lease agreements on major fixed assets, like production machinery or buildings. Though the related assets aren't technically owned by the corporation, they show up in the fixed asset section of the balance sheet.
- **Retirement Benefits Payable:** If a corporation offers a pension plan, the money it's expected to pay out to current and future retirees is a corporate liability.
- **Contingent Liabilities:** Contingent liabilities are *possibilities* rather than done deals, so they show up in the footnotes to the financial statements instead of on the balance sheet. They include things like unsettled lawsuits and warranties (promises to repair or replace defective products). For example, if a company sold a refrigerator with a two-year warranty, it would owe the *possible* expense of covering any necessary repairs or replacements until the two-year term expired.

Notes payable and bonds payable are both financing debts, meaning they're used to finance things like expansion plans and acquisitions (such as new factories or other companies), and they come with interest payable on top of the original principle balances. Capital lease obligations and retirement benefits payable are operating liabilities, meaning that they arise out of normal business activity.

Total liabilities for a company offset its total assets, formalized in the accounting equation, to determine that company's equity—what it's *really* worth.

EQUITY

Mine, All Mine

When you first start a business, you (along with any co-owners) typically put some of your own assets into the company. Those original contributions form the first entries in your equity account, and get your business on its way. Adding resources into the company is one way to beef up your equity account, whether those resources come from you and other involved owners or from silent investors.

Any asset you personally put into the business increases your equity stake. The most commonly contributed asset is money, but all other personal assets that are used exclusively by the company count as well. Contributed assets can be anything from a laptop computer to a backyard shed to a pickup truck that now bears your company logo. For major assets like that pickup truck, it's important to retitle the asset in the company name to avoid any problems down the line, such as the IRS questioning ownership (after all, you can't claim depreciation expense on a personal vehicle).

Negative Equity

It's not uncommon for new companies to end up with negative equity after their first year or two in business. This happens when early losses are greater than the initial capital investment. It indicates the business is struggling, but things can turn around with workable ideas for boosting revenues.

Equity represents how much of your company is really yours, and not owed to someone else. Think of it the way you think about your house:

You may own your house, but the bank probably has a claim on part of it, too, in the form of your mortgage. Here, your house is your asset, your mortgage is your liability, and the part of your house that you truly own (the difference between its value and your outstanding mortgage balance) is your equity. It's exactly the same for business. You have your assets, you owe your liabilities, and you own your equity stake.

EQUITY SPLIT

The main split among equity accounts, common to all business types, is in which direction the capital is flowing. There are:

- Equity contributions, which means owners put more of their own cash into the company.
- Equity withdrawals, which means owners take money out of the company, but not as regular salary.
- Current profit or loss that becomes a permanent piece of the equity account. As you might expect, profits increase equity, while losses decrease it.

The best way to grow the equity of a company is to keep some of the profits that the company earns inside the business. Many small business owners like to take out profits as soon as they're earned. After all, they've had to pay tax on the money, and they want to enjoy the benefits of the money they earned. If you're planning to expand your company, though, leaving some of those profits inside is a great first step toward growth. It can also make your company more attractive to prospective lenders, as banks are often more likely to make a loan when they see there is substantial equity at stake.

WHICH KIND OF EQUITY IS IT?

When it comes to business, equity comes with a bit of a twist. Though equity is about ownership no matter what type of company you have, the accounts you use depend entirely on your business structure. Different business structures include:

- Sole proprietorships
- Partnerships
- Limited liability companies (LLCs)
- S corporations
- C corporations

The structure of your company dictates how the equity looks for accounting purposes, and exactly what types of equity accounts that appear in your books.

Sole proprietorships and partnerships have a separate owner's equity (or capital) account for each owner, along with a corresponding withdrawal account for each. The owner's equity account is a permanent account, and contributions are made directly into this account. The withdrawal accounts are temporary and are folded into the owner's equity account at the end of the accounting period, along with that period's net profit or loss.

Corporations don't have equity accounts directly geared toward individual owners. Instead, they have accounts for each type of stock they issue to represent the contributed capital, plus a special account called "additional paid-in capital" (for contributions greater than the par value of the stock). Unlike sole proprietorships and partnerships, no other accounts are folded into these. Earnings at the end of the period are held in the retained earnings account. Owner withdrawals are a much more formal affair, and here they exist only in the form of dividends. The dividends account is temporary, and is rolled into retained earnings at the end of the period.

AN OVERLOOKED STATEMENT CLEARS THINGS UP

Along with the big three financial statements (the balance sheet, the statement of profit and loss, and the statement of cash flows), there's a fourth less often used report called the statement of changes in owner's equity. This report walks readers through how the equity has grown (or decreased) during the fiscal period (the same period used for the statement of profit and loss).

This simple, short statement starts with the opening value of owner's equity (whatever form it takes) from the beginning of the period. Next, the document lists the changes to equity, adding the increases and subtracting the decreases. Increases include net profits and capital contributions; decreases include losses and owner withdrawals. The bottom line of this statement gives you the current balance of the owner's equity. That presents a complete picture of the true value of the company; its net worth. The most important way a company can grow its net worth comes from the results of its operations, in the form of (hopefully) profits.

Chapter 5

Revenues, Costs, and Expenses

New and small business owners tend to track their profit-related accounts very closely. There's a good reason for this: Without pretty consistent profits, no business can survive for the long haul. Three numbers go into figuring out profits: revenues, costs, and expenses. Every business has revenues (hopefully) and expenses (definitely). Only product-based businesses have costs. In the profit equation, you start with revenues, then deduct costs and expenses. When the result is positive, you have profits. When it's negative, your company has sustained a loss for the period.

In the profit equation, a product-based company with costs will see an additional and crucial subtotal called gross profit (when expressed as a percentage, it's called gross margin). That number represents the revenue left over once you take out the direct costs of the products you are selling. The gross profit tells you how much you have available to cover all the rest of your expenses, ideally leaving some net profit at the end.

In this chapter, you'll learn everything you need to know about revenues, costs, and expenses, from setting appropriate prices to monitoring and managing product costs to tracking the daily operating expenses. How well a company manages these three income components determines whether they'll enjoy net profits, or suffer net losses.

REVENUES

Let's Make a Deal

The goal of every small business is to rack up revenues (also called sales). After all, revenues are the first step on the path to profits. When it comes to recording revenues for accounting purposes, though, it's not quite as simple as just ringing up a sale. There are different types of sales transactions, and different accounting methods to use. With all the variables surrounding a single sales transaction, the accounting can seem overwhelming, but each transaction really involves just a few basic steps to get the entry recorded and your business another step closer to profitability.

Before you can record that transaction, though, you have to have something to sell, set prices, and attract potential customers. Here, you'll learn just how to do all of that.

THE PRICE IS RIGHT

There are two components that go into your gross profit (also called the gross margin). The first is the price you charge your customers for a product, and the second is the amount it costs you to buy that product from your supplier, or what it costs you in time and effort to supply a service. The difference between price and cost is the gross profit.

While you do have some control over costs, such as switching vendors or revisiting employee pay, that control is somewhat limited. Prices, on the other hand, are set completely at your discretion. The bigger the gap between your price and your cost, the higher your gross profit will be. The trick is to set your prices as high as possible without scaring off your customers; after all, sales at slightly lower prices are much better than no sales at all.

To figure out how much of your sales are going toward general expenses and profits, you can divide your gross profit by your sales to calculate the gross margin percentage. Here's an example: Suppose your monthly sales are $20,000 and your costs are $15,000. That would give you a gross profit of $5,000 ($20,000 minus $15,000). Now take that gross profit of $5,000 and divide it by the sales of $20,000 to get your gross margin percentage; in this case, 25 percent. That means 25 percent of every sales dollar is available to cover all of your business expenses.

Gross margin percentages tend to vary widely by industry. Some industries have very high margins of more than 50 percent; others have very tight margins of 10 to 15 percent. It really depends on the item you're selling, and how much markup customers are willing to bear. For example, the margin on luxury items is normally much higher than the margin on groceries.

If you are in a low-margin industry, it means you can't really set your prices too high above your costs or you'll risk losing a lot of sales. In that case, keeping a close eye on expenses is a good way to ensure bottom-line profitability. The other way toward profitability is to generate a very high level of sales volume, but that can be harder to pull off. Especially for new or small businesses, strict expense management can make all the difference between profits and losses.

THE BASICS OF SALES TRANSACTIONS

Every sales transaction increases your company's revenues, and recording those transactions gets you one step closer to seeing your net profits. There is one thing all sales transactions have in common from an accounting perspective: a credit entry to the sales account. The rest depends on the particular circumstances surrounding the transaction, and there can be a bit of variation in those circumstances. Accounting software has made all of this much easier to deal with; in fact, most of the transaction details will be invisible to you. But having a thorough understanding of how things work behind the scenes can offer you valuable insights on the best ways to manage sales.

For instance, the way your company makes sales has an impact on your transactions. Sales can be made for cash, resulting in a debit to cash; or on credit, resulting in a debit to accounts receivable. Then there's the "when" factor to consider: Companies using the cash method of accounting only record sales when actual cash is received, whereas companies using the accrual method have to record sales in the moment, regardless of payment. Finally, if your company sells products, the inventory method you've chosen plays a big part in transactions as well. If your company uses a perpetual inventory system (where you subtract every item from the inventory account as soon as you sell it, which makes sense if you're selling unique products, have limited inventory, or use barcode scanning software to ring up each sale), every entry for a product sale must have a corresponding entry for cost of goods sold. Under a periodic inventory system (where you only make entries to the inventory account periodically, such as once a month), though, no cost of goods entries are recorded during the accounting period, resulting in a single-entry sales transaction. This method would make more sense for companies that have very large inventory or sell indistinguishable products (such as nails and screws).

The Deciding Factor

Remember, companies with inventory generally must use the accrual method of accounting. Even if your business sells a combination of goods and services, the inventory issue is the deciding factor. That means every sale—even if a sale doesn't involve any inventory—has to be recorded, whether or not you've been paid yet.

The method variables (inventory system and accounting method) are stable factors. Once you've chosen a method, it dictates that part of the entry every time. For example, if you use the cash method, you cannot ever record a sales transaction until you've been paid. Under a perpetual inventory system, you have to book a cost of goods transaction for every single inventory item you sell. The cash or credit issue may vary, because it depends on the actual sales transactions.

COLLECTING SALES TAX

If you sell products, you probably will have to deal with sales tax. In fact, even if you provide only services to your customers, you may still have to deal with sales tax, though that's still more the exception than the rule. Either way, sales tax tends to be pretty straightforward:

you collect it from customers, then send it in to the state along with a brief sales tax return. Sales tax requirements vary from state to state, and are sometimes linked with total revenues, but most require monthly or quarterly filings.

The Sales Tax Effect

Sales tax is a state issue, and you can find out about applicable sales tax requirements by contacting your state's revenue collection office. They'll tell you which items are subject to sales tax, how much you have to collect, which forms to fill out, and when you have to send it all in.

From an accounting perspective, the sales tax that you get from customers has nothing to do with revenues, and the sales tax that you pay to the state has nothing to do with expenses. Yes, you collect sales tax as part of a sales transaction, but that part of the transaction has absolutely no impact on your statement of profit and loss. Instead, this is a balance-sheet-only transaction affecting two accounts: sales tax payable and cash. At the time of sale, you debit the cash account and credit sales tax payable as part of the overall sales transaction; when you send in the payment, you debit sales tax payable and credit cash, just as you would for any other payable account.

So you see that sales tax payable gets recorded at the time of the sale, and that sales tax must be paid in accordance with state guidelines, which happens whether or not your company has actually been paid yet by the customer.

CASH VERSUS CREDIT

Pay Now or Pay Later?

There are two major differences between cash sales and credit sales: timing and risk. With a cash sale, you get paid on the spot with money, checks, or credit cards; with credit sales, where your company extends the credit, you get a promise that your company will be paid sometime in the future. Cash sales provide differing levels of risk, ranging from none for actual cash to possible risk for credit card sales and customer checks. On top of that, there's the potential for losing a sale, or even losing a new customer, as some will only make purchases when they can pay later. For example, if your small business sells business cards and brochures to other small companies, they may expect thirty-day payment terms; if you don't offer those terms, and insist on cash up front, they may take their business elsewhere. With credit sales, though, you run the risk that the customer won't pay on time, or that the customer won't pay you at all.

For some new business owners, it can be tempting to extend credit left and right to attract customers and increase sales to get that business off the ground. Others are afraid to extend credit at all, and only make cash sales to make sure they'll have enough money to meet expenses as they come due. After being in business for a while, the two styles usually meld, resulting in a sort of cash-credit combination. For example, you might have a client pay 50 percent up front before you create their advertising campaign, and collect the balance 30 days after delivery.

SIMPLE CASH SALES

Cash sales, which include every sale in which the customer pays right away, even if it's by check or credit card, are easier to record than credit sales in two very important ways:

1. First, you don't have to bother recording the transaction in a specific customer's account on top of the general account.
2. Second, there's no second step to the transaction. (With credit sales, you have a second transaction to record when the cash is finally received.)

Plus, it doesn't matter whether you use the accrual method or the cash method: When you have a straight cash transaction, you record it right there and then.

Keeping Things Simple

The easiest way to track your cash sales is to deposit every penny you receive, whether the customer pays with cash, check, or credit card. This way, your revenues equal your deposits, which simplifies recordkeeping.

In the past, cash sales were recorded in one giant journal entry at the end of each day. Now, with software and apps, credit card and check sales are recorded automatically as they happen; only actual cash money sales may need to be accounted for manually. Your accounting software has a special journal for these transactions called (not surprisingly) the cash receipts journal.

To keep your bookkeeping job as simple as possible, make sure your deposit slips match your journal entries exactly. If you record $862 in cash sales on Monday, deposit $862 on Tuesday. That way you have an easily traced trail from your sales to your bank deposits, which can come in handy should any questions arise.

CREDIT SALES

When you extend credit to your customers there will be a lag between the time of the sale and the time you get paid. Credit sales by nature allow customers to buy now and pay later. You'll present the customer with an invoice detailing the transaction, and the customer will offer you the implicit promise to make payment on some later agreed-upon date.

The basic journal entry, which will be recorded in your sales journal, is fairly simple: a debit to accounts receivable, and a credit to sales. Unlike cash sales, you cannot record credit sales in one big lump; they must be recorded individually so you can properly account for each customer's purchases.

To keep track of individual customers' accounts, accounting software offers a customer ledger (also called an accounts receivable subledger). The sum of all your individual customer balances is held in (and must equal the balance in) the main accounts receivable account in the general ledger.

RECEIPTS VERSUS INVOICES

Whether you offer credit or make cash sales only, when you complete a sale transaction you need to make a record of it. With a cash sale, the standard source document (where you can find the details of the transaction) is the sales receipt, which contains such information as the date, amount, and description of what was sold. For credit sales (not credit card sales; those are treated like cash sales), the source document is an invoice. Invoices include all the same information as sales receipts, plus a bit more, such as:

- Customer name and contact information
- Customer account number
- Credit terms and due date
- Customer's purchase order number (where applicable)
- Invoice number

To keep your records straight, it's better to use prenumbered sales receipts and invoices, making sure to use them in order. Doing so makes for much easier tracking, both when you create the invoice and down the line.

Whether your company collects immediate cash or extends credit, every sale you make increases your revenue account. And all the product costs and sales expenses involved in making that sale must also be accounted for.

And Then There Are Statements

A customer statement is a document containing summary information for that customer's account. It includes a listing of all transactions for the period, such as new invoices and payments received. The statement ends with a balance due, which is the total amount you expect to receive from that customer.

THE COST-INVENTORY CONNECTION

From the Shelf to the Shopping Bag

Whether you are a manufacturer, a wholesaler, or a retailer, your business sells some kind of product. When you sell products of any kind, first you have to create or buy them. The products you have on hand, the ones that you intend to sell directly to your customers, make up your inventory asset. Your inventory can include finished merchandise (such as a desk), raw materials (wood to make the desk), or anything in between. If your company makes products, you are a manufacturer, and your inventory has to go through a few steps before it makes its journey to the sales floor.

Costs Aren't Expenses?

It's very easy to confuse costs and expenses; after all, they seem like the same thing. In accounting, costs refer to the amount of money you have to spend to buy or make a product that you plan to sell to someone else. Expenses, on the other hand, exist whether or not you buy or make or sell anything.

As soon as you sell one of your products, it stops being part of your inventory and turns into a special kind of business expense known as cost of goods sold. At that point, it also makes the transformation from a balance sheet item to a piece of the profit-and-loss puzzle. In accounting, though, the conversion of inventory to cost of goods may not show up in the books immediately, depending on the inventory system you choose to use.

In this chapter, you'll learn all about how your cost of goods will help you set your prices, what exactly should go into your cost category, and the four different ways to compute the value of your inventory once you know exactly how much you have on hand.

COSTS HELP YOU SET PRICES

With product-based businesses, you need to know your inventory costs before setting prices. Those costs should be starting points, but many new business owners use these alone as a basis to set prices. For new small business owners, figuring out the complete costs of what's being sold can be difficult and time-consuming, which leads many to just use their best guesses. However, not knowing the true costs can result in significantly underpricing products and services, which ultimately leads to losses and possibly even business failure.

Here are the three things that the price of a good needs to cover:

1. The immediate cost of what you're selling
2. A portion of both your selling expenses and your general expenses
3. A reasonable profit left over for you

Here's an example of how these three things factor into pricing. Let's say you're selling desk sets that you bought for $50. You also had to advertise the desk sets, have a place to store them, have an employee to ring up the sale, put the desk set in a shopping bag, and pay overhead expenses (like electricity). So you'd need to figure out an appropriate proportion of those costs, let's say $4 per desk set (a made-up number here) to add to the $50 actual product cost. On top of that, you need to add a reasonable profit so that your company could make money; let's say $5 per desk set. That would mean you would sell each desk set for $59. If you left out any of those factors, you could lose money on every single sale, or simply break even and not make any profits.

When you're working out the numbers, make sure to include every component of cost of goods sold. As for your desired net profits, which are the whole point of the sales, adding on a reasonable percentage for your industry makes a good starting point. For example, someone selling unique designer dresses could expect to see a higher profit percentage on each individual sale than someone selling one-size-fits-all rain boots.

How Low Can You Go?

The price floor is the absolute minimum at which you can set your prices without sustaining losses on every single sale. The price ceiling is the absolute maximum price the market will bear. The price you charge for your products or services will usually fall somewhere in the middle.

WHAT GOES INTO INVENTORY COSTS?

The whole point of having your inventory is selling it. The point of selling it is to make some money. In order to actually make a profit by selling your inventory, you have to know how much it *really* costs to make every item so you can set your prices accordingly. Otherwise, you could actually lose money on every single product you sell.

For retailers and wholesalers who buy and sell complete merchandise, that total cost isn't too hard to figure out, though it's a little more involved than you may think. Manufacturers—companies that actually make the products from scratch—have a lot more math to do to get to their true inventory costs.

Retailers

In the retail trade, you get merchandise from your suppliers and sell it as is to your customers. If it comes in a box, you sell it in the box; if it comes blue, you sell it blue. Still, you do have a few numbers to add up to get to your total product cost. At the base of this calculation is the price you paid for the product. Add to that any sales tax you had to pay, plus any delivery charges you paid to get the product to you. If you got some kind of discount, deduct that from your inventory cost. Now, you have the basic equation:

Total inventory cost = total item price + sales tax + delivery charges – discounts

Doing that calculation gives you the *real* cost of every inventory item, and gives you better information for setting prices that will result in profits.

Manufacturers

When your company makes the products that it sells, figuring out the product costs takes some work. First, you need to know exactly what went into making the product. Second, you need to know how much you paid for each component that goes into the finished product. This part works the same way as it does for retail goods; you add up the item cost, the sales tax paid, and any delivery charges, and subtract any discount you received.

Since you are creating new products out of the component parts, though, you have another couple of steps to tackle. You also have to figure out how much labor goes into making each product, and tack that on to the cost. Plus, any overhead costs associated with production—like rent and utilities for a workshop—gets factored into inventory costs as well. This is where accounting software takes over the heavy lifting, calculating how much of each cost component goes with each item in inventory.

FOUR WAYS TO VALUE INVENTORY

Whether your company makes products or simply sells them, you need to consider the best way to track the value of your inventory for accounting purposes. Using the method that most closely matches the flow of your sales will give you the clearest picture of that inventory's true value.

There are four ways to track the value of inventory under U.S. GAAP (Generally Accepted Accounting Principles):

- Last in, first out (LIFO): The last product you buy is the one you sell first (a method only allowed in the U.S., used to lower net income and income taxes) in a period of rising product costs.
- First in, first out (FIFO): The first item you buy is the first one sold, which works well, from a tax and accounting perspective, when product costs are steadily falling.

- Average cost: Works well when selling a large number of identical items (like hammers) that your company has purchased at different times for different prices.
- Specific identification: Usually used for big ticket or unique goods, like paintings or cars.

The valuation method that works best for your business depends on what type of inventory you keep. When you offer more than one kind of product for sale you can use a different inventory valuation method for each, because what makes sense for one product may seem somewhat ridiculous for the other. For example, if you own a hardware store, you might use average cost for things like nails and screws, specific identification for custom sheds, and either LIFO or FIFO for things like snow shovels and leaf blowers.

The reason you need to choose a method in the first place is because you buy inventory at different times throughout the year, and items may not cost the exact same amount every time. Unless every single item you sell is tagged with a unique identifier (which can be cost prohibitive if you carry a lot of inventory), you really have no way of knowing exactly which piece of inventory was sold—one nail looks exactly like every other nail. So you have to come up with a way to best estimate the cost of the inventory that's been sold during the period.

Because different methods will give you different outcomes, prevailing accounting principles make you pick a method and stick with it. If you need to make a change, you have to have a good reason (based on FASB and IRS guidelines). You also may have to recalculate prior years' numbers to show the impact of the change, and you have to stick with the new method going forward. You cannot keep switching your inventory valuation method to make your numbers come out better.

EXPENSES

We All Have Bills to Pay

One of the oldest business clichés says that you have to spend money to make money. Expenses are the standard costs of operating a business (like rent, electricity, and advertising), and there's really no way around them.

Unlike your personal expenses, every business expense is tax-deductible, at least to some degree. The list of what counts as a business expense is vast, and, as you'll see in this entry, includes some things you wouldn't expect. Having a good working knowledge of business expenses will help you develop a better picture of your company's profitability, and help you manage your tax bill. It can also save you some money: When you know what your accountant will be looking for when he does your taxes, you can come in completely prepared.

More important, how you manage expenses has an enormous impact on your company's bottom line. If your business isn't netting a profit, or the profits don't seem big enough, taking a hard look at the expenses is the first place to start searching for ways to improve profitability. Keep in mind that expense accounts all have normal debit balances, which is the exact opposite of standard revenue accounts. In fact, there are very few times when you will ever see a credit entry in an expense account. Those rare occasions would be to correct mistakes, to reverse an accrual from an earlier period, or to close out the account. Any other credit postings are probably mistakes, which you need to correct by adjusting entries.

Like most everything else in accounting, there are so many different expenses that it's easier to group them than it is to look at one very long list. The most common division is between sell-ing expenses and overhead, which is typically called "general and administrative" expenses on financial statements.

Remember, costs directly associated with inventory don't count as expenses. Expenses only include bills you'd have to pay whether or not you ever sold anything.

Tracking Is Optional

There is no accounting rule that requires you to split out your selling costs. If selling costs don't make up a large part of your total expenses, you can leave them in with your general expenses. However, if they are high enough for you to want to track them separately, you can make a selling costs category within your general expenses.

SELLING COSTS

Selling costs include any expense involved in selling your products or services that tie in directly with sales. For example, sales com-missions would count as a selling cost, and so would receipt paper, gift wrap, and delivery charges (when you deliver something to your customers). Those types of costs don't exist without sales, so they vary directly with your sales.

Examples of direct selling costs include:

- Shopping bags
- Gift boxes and wrapping
- Packaging materials
- Delivery fees

- Order fulfillment costs
- Sales commissions

These direct costs are also called variable costs because the total monthly expense *varies* based on sales.

Indirect selling costs are those expenses that are necessary to generate sales but don't vary based on sales. Basically, your company has to pay for these expenses even if you don't sell a single thing. However, it can be nearly impossible to generate sales without these indirect selling costs, making them well worth the cost. The most common indirect selling costs include sales salaries, advertising expenses, promotional costs, and travel. Essentially, any cost you incur while trying to convince customers to buy your product can count in this expense category. You may include meals and entertainment here as well; many business owners take clients and potential clients for lunch or drinks, or conduct business over rounds of golf.

Working on Commission

Don't confuse sales salaries with sales commissions. Sales salaries are paid to the sales staff regularly, regardless of whether they generate sales or how much they sell. Commissions are only paid when a sale has been made: No sales means no commissions.

When you choose to highlight your selling costs separately, they will be the first expenses listed on your statement of profit and loss. That's because they are more closely linked to sales than are your other expenses, and so they appear on the statement closer to the revenue section.

OVERHEAD

A lot of people throw around the term "overhead" without really knowing what it means. It's often considered a catchall for anything that's not a direct product cost (the actual cost of the products plus related selling expenses), and that's partly correct. Sometimes it's called fixed expenses, and that's also only partly correct. The true definition is this: Overhead includes any expense your company would incur even if it never sold anything. Those expenses could be exactly the same every month, or they might never be the same; they're fixed in the sense that you have to pay them to stay in business, but the dollar amount can change. What overhead does not include are direct and indirect product costs—anything that varies in relation to sales.

This category is where you'll find the unexpected expenses, things you may not think are tax deductible. Here are some of the most common overhead expenses that new and small business owners forget to include:

- Business-related books and magazines (one-time purchase and subscriptions)
- Donations (such as providing T-shirts for a softball team)
- Tolls, parking, and mileage (for any business travel, no matter how far)
- Professional dues (association memberships, for example)

Some overhead expenses come with special rules, courtesy of the IRS. Of these, the two most likely to impact your small business are home office and entertainment expenses. Others, such as depreciation and amortization expenses and payroll, come with a side order of math.

Home Office Expenses

Many new and small business owners do at least part of their work from home. If you were to rent office space, all of the expenses associated with that would be fully deductible overhead expenses; the home office deduction lets you record the same types of expenses for your business. However, you can only deduct part of the total expense, because part of your home is for personal use. Typically, your deductions can include a portion of your mortgage interest and property taxes, rent payments, utilities (not including a primary home phone, if you have one), security system, insurance, and general maintenance and repairs.

Home Office Tax Deduction

You can only use the home office deduction if you file a Schedule C for your business income. That form is for sole proprietors and single-member LLCs only. For other business types, the associated expenses may be included with the company's regular expenses. Talk to your accountant for advice on how to treat these expenses.

In order to qualify for this deduction, you have to use part of your home regularly and exclusively for business purposes. You also have to use that spot as your principal place of business for whatever tasks you do there; for example, if you always do your billing from home, that counts. It also counts if you normally meet with customers there, or if it's actually a separate structure on the same property (such as a shed or guest house).

Once your home office qualifies, you have to figure out how big it is in relation to the rest of your house. You can do that using square-foot measurements. For example, if your workspace is 100 square feet and your whole home is 1,000 square feet, you can deduct 10 percent of the common expenses. Expenses that apply only to the office space (such as special wiring or repainting) will be 100 percent deductible. Expenses that don't apply to that space at all—for instance, the cost of painting your kid's bedroom—aren't deductible.

Entertainment Expenses

When you're schmoozing vendors, wooing clients, or doing something special for employees, the associated costs fall under overhead. These entertainment expenses come with a lot of limitations. To start, they have to be considered "ordinary and necessary" for your business. Also, you can only deduct half of the total expense when you take clients out to lunch. Small gifts, $25 or less per person your company gives a gift to, can be fully deductible, though—and can make just as big an impression on your customers as a more expensive gift.

The Gift Loophole

Here's an entertainment loophole: Give gifts to a company instead of to a person. When you do that, the gifts are 100 percent deductible, with no $25 limit. Instead of giving five guys $60 theater tickets and only getting a $125 deduction, give the tickets to a company and deduct the full $300.

As you might expect, these types of expenses are audit favorites, so save your receipts and document the business purpose whenever possible. Even if you lose track of some, you'll likely be able to keep the deduction if the lost receipts were for less than $75 each, a fairly new easing of the IRS receipt rules. You are, however, *required* to keep an entertainment expense log that includes the date, place, dollar amount, client name, and business purpose of each event.

DON'T LOSE YOUR RECEIPTS

When tax time rolls around, many small business owners begin searching everywhere for receipts and invoices not yet accounted for. They try to remember every trip they made in the name of the company, every meeting they attended, every client lunch. They do this to make sure that every one of their expenses makes it into the accounting records for the year, and for good reason: Every dollar of expense translates into a reduction of income, and less income means a lower tax bill.

More things count as deductible expenses than you might think. For example, if you have to take courses to maintain a professional license, save the invoices and deduct those fees. When you drive to visit customer sites, every mile you travel goes toward deductible expenses (the mileage rate varies from year to year based on federal law). Other commonly overlooked business expenses include reference books, alarm systems, bank charges, and dry-cleaning of uniforms.

Be aware that business meals and entertainment expenses may not be 100 percent deductible for tax purposes. Be careful, too, not to go overboard with these social expenses. This is an area more closely monitored by the IRS than others, because there can be a fine line between the personal and the business aspects of these expenses. While traveling to Hawaii to meet with a store owner who may begin stocking your sunglasses counts as business travel, staying an extra two weeks and bringing the whole family along does not.

DEPRECIATION

More Than Wear and Tear

Depreciation, as we discussed briefly in Chapter 4, is the accounting way of measuring the wear and tear on your fixed assets. Though it has no impact on cash, it is part of your expenses. That means depreciation lowers your company's net income, which also means a lower income tax bill. Unlike expenses, when you buy assets you don't get to deduct them right away, even though they have taken up a portion of your cash or increased your liabilities. Taking depreciation expense allows you to deduct that asset over time, as you use it to help produce revenues. Here we'll get into the nitty-gritty details of calculating and recording depreciation expense for your company's fixed assets.

Take It All Right Now

You can fully depreciate newly acquired assets immediately by using the Section 179 deduction. Instead of depreciating assets over time, you can expense the total fixed assets purchased during the year. Two catches: the deduction can't cause an overall loss, and it can't be more than the IRS limit for that tax year.

Though there are several different ways to depreciate assets, the two most often used by small businesses are:

1. Modified Accelerated Cost Recovery System, or MACRS method (also called the tax method)
2. The straight-line method

Both methods are acceptable for use on your business tax return. Although you can use one method for book purposes and another for tax purposes (and you have to report that fact to the IRS), it's easier to keep your books and tax records the same way. The main difference is that MACRS lets you take bigger depreciation deductions *sooner* than you would using the straight-line method (that's where the "accelerated" comes from); overall, though, the total depreciation over the life of the asset will be the same.

Whichever method you choose, you'll need some basic pieces of information to get started: the asset cost, purchase date, useful life, and what percentage the asset is used exclusively for the business. If the asset won't be used 100 percent by the business, you can only depreciate the portion used by the company. For example, if you have a laptop that you use both for business and personal reasons, you must estimate the percentage of business use; if the business use is 80 percent, you can only deduct 80 percent of that year's total depreciation calculation for the business.

Let's take a closer look at each type of method.

MACRS DEPRECIATION

MACRS is what the IRS wants businesses to use for calculating depreciation. Under this method, all assets are lumped into categories called property classes, and each property class comes with a specific depreciation schedule. For example, all office furniture is considered seven-year property, while all computers are considered five-year property. Each property class comes with its own preset annual expense percentages schedule (the percentages change every year). You can download a complete copy of the table from the

IRS website (www.irs.gov). The MACRS asset categories and depreciation schedules are surprisingly clear and simple to use.

In most cases, you'll use the "half-year convention" table. The basic point of this table is to help you properly calculate depreciation, because no business buys all of its assets on January 1. The half-year convention assumes that all new assets were purchased at mid-year, and gives them all 50 percent of the full depreciation for the first year; it then allows for the full-year expense going forward. You'll notice that the tables have an extra year built in; three-year assets have four years of percentages, for example. That's to account for the half year at the end of the asset's life to make up for the missing half year at the beginning.

Here's how MACRS depreciation works. First, you figure out which category your asset belongs in, according to the IRS chart. Then you look up the percentage for this year in the asset's life. For instance, if it's the second tax year you have the asset, use the percentage for year two. Finally, you multiply the total original asset cost by the percentage from the chart. If the asset isn't used exclusively for business, you have to take an extra step and multiply the business-use percentage by the depreciation amount you just calculated.

Keeping It Straight

When it's allowed, a lot of new business owners prefer to use straight-line depreciation for asset purchases. That's because new businesses often sustain losses early on, and bigger depreciation deductions using MACRS aren't necessary to keep income taxes low. In later years, when profits start growing, the extra depreciation expense amount generated using the straight-line method helps keep the tax bill to a minimum.

STRAIGHT-LINE DEPRECIATION

Straight-line depreciation is usually an acceptable option for most assets, even though the IRS prefers MACRS. Though this method gives you a lower depreciation expense up-front, the annual deduction remains steady over the life of the asset. This method also gives you bigger deductions than MACRS in later years.

The calculation for straight-line depreciation is straightforward. Take the total original cost of the asset and divide that by the asset's useful life (usually taken from the MACRS asset class listing). The result is the annual depreciation expense, which is the number you'll use every year except the first and last. For those years, you can go with 50 percent, to mimic the half-year convention, or you can figure out the true proportion, what percentage of the year you actually owned the asset. For example, if you bought the asset in February, you could multiply the total expense by $^{10}/_{12}$ because your company will have used the asset for 10 out of 12 months during the first year; you would use 10 instead of 11 because March would be the first full month the asset was in use.

DON'T FORGET AMORTIZATION

Amortization expense is similar to depreciation, except it's only used for intangible assets. This expense measures decline in the value of those assets over time. How do intangible assets decline in value? Well, they don't wear out or rust, but some of them, such as patents, have specific end dates. Others, such as licensing agreements, come with clear useful lives. Also, according to IRS regulations, a company can't amortize an intangible asset (like a copyright or patent) that it created, only those that it purchased.

The running total of amortization expense is sometimes (but not always) held in a contra account, which generally is called accumulated amortization. The reasoning here is the same as it is for depreciation: This allows you to see the original value of the asset separately from how much of it has been "used up." For amortization, though, you actually have another choice, which you don't have for depreciation: You can record amortization directly to the intangible asset account instead of using the contra account, saving you extra bookkeeping work at the end of the accounting period.

Unlike depreciation, amortization can only be calculated on a straight-line basis. That means for each period the exact same amount is booked to expense until it's all used up. If your company bought a patent for $15,000 that had 15 years left until expiration, you would amortize $1,000 per year for 15 years.

Maximum Life

You can't amortize any intangible asset over more than 15 years, even if it has a much longer legal or useful life. If the asset's useful or legal life is shorter than 15 years, though, you have to use that shorter time span when you figure out the expense.

Though it may seem as though amortization won't apply to your company, it probably will. The most common amortization expense for small business is startup costs. While you're doing all the things you have to do to get your business started, there's no actual business for which you can deduct those expenses. Instead, you have to lump the expenses into an asset, and amortize them over five years. Expenses you would typically put into this account include legal fees, business licenses, and incorporation fees (or the equivalent for LLCs or partnerships)—any expense you incur to create the company.

PEOPLE AND PAYROLL

It's Payday!

Payroll is one of the most involved and time-consuming aspects of accounting, and it looks pretty complicated at first glance. Once you get through the initial setup and get the hang of it, though, payroll is really not so tough. Yes, there is a lot of paperwork. But much of the paperwork is fairly repetitive, and it will become routine before you know it. And with the software and apps available today, payroll is easier to manage than ever before. Still, there are a lot of filing deadlines, and stiff penalties for missing them. It's often easier (and not too expensive) to hire an accountant or payroll service to take care of it for you.

Employees are often the single biggest expense a company can have. First, you have to pay them, and that's usually a big expense in itself. On top of that, though, your business is responsible for extra taxes and some insurance. Finally, your company has to comply with all local, state, and federal requirements, most of which are in place to protect your employees, and some come with a price tag. To escape the extra costs and responsibilities that come with employees, a lot of new and small businesses enlist independent contractors. This strategy can save you a lot of money and a lot of headaches. But beware: there are both advantages and potential pitfalls when using independent contractors instead of employees. What else do you need to know about payroll? Read on!

A LOT OF WORK AND FORMS

Having employees can be pretty time-consuming all around and paying them is no different. You have to deal with state and federal taxes, multiple report filings, unemployment insurance, and a whole lot more. Even if you have only one employee, you have to fill out every form and meet every filing deadline.

Once you have the basics covered, you can use your accounting software to help you manage payroll. Most of these software programs come with a payroll module, and the rest often provide an add-on program that interconnects with the standard software. Using accounting software is by far the easiest and quickest way to do your own payroll. The setup is the most labor-intensive part, but even that takes less time than you would imagine. Once that's done, your part will be limited to telling the program everyone's gross pay. The software can do all the rest. It will calculate every deduction, figure out the take-home pay, keep track of the tax payments you (as the employer) have to make, and even print out the paychecks. Before you get started cranking out the paychecks, though, there are several important steps you have to take.

PAYROLL BASICS

You've probably gotten a paycheck at some point in your life, and were as dismayed as everyone else when you realized how much money was taken out. Now you will be the one taking the money out and sending it to the tax men. In addition, employers have to kick in more payroll taxes on top of the ones they deduct from employee paychecks.

As the employer, you have to account for two sets of taxes:

1. The **withholding taxes** are the employee's own income taxes, taken directly out of their paychecks and sent to the tax office (by you). Withholding taxes include income tax (always federal, usually state, and sometimes local), Social Security, and Medicare.
2. The **employer taxes** are additional taxes that you have to pay on behalf of your employees, and they include Social Security and Medicare as well as any state and federal unemployment insurance payments.

Yes, there are a lot of taxes, a lot of calculations, and a lot of paperwork. On the plus side, the payroll grand total is deductible from your company's income, lowering the company's income tax burden.

WITHHOLDING TAXES

Again, any tax you deduct from an employee's paycheck is called a withholding tax. The four most common withholding taxes are:

1. Federal income tax
2. State income tax
3. Social Security
4. Medicare

In some states, you may also have to withhold unemployment or disability insurance from employee pay.

In order to figure out how much to deduct for income taxes, you need to know some basic information about each employee. That includes his marital status and the number of allowances he's claiming, both of which you can get from the W-4 form that the employee completes. You also need to know his gross salary for the period and the amount of any pretax deductions.

Pretax Deductions

Pretax deductions are subtracted from your employees' gross pay *before* you figure out how much income tax to withhold. Common examples include retirement plan contributions and health insurance premiums. Suppose Mary earns $250 per week. If she pays $10 to her 401(k) and $20 toward health insurance, then you would calculate her income tax withholding on $220 instead of $250.

How often you need to file a payroll tax return and remit federal payroll taxes depends on the amount of the payroll tax liability. In most cases, you will need to deposit federal payroll taxes using electronic funds transfer (EFT); very small companies with payroll tax liabilities less than $2,500 per quarter *may* be allowed to file quarterly payroll tax returns and submit payment with them. The rules involving federal payroll taxes are very strict and detailed. To make sure you are handling them properly, read IRS Publication 15 at www.irs.gov.

Never Screw Around with Payroll Taxes

One common and potentially business-crushing mistake made by new employers is using withholding taxes as a business bank account. Rather than making payroll tax deposits in full and on time, they cover their other cash-flow gaps by borrowing from the payroll tax account. Doing that is 100 percent illegal, and the penalties are pretty stiff, often enough to put small businesses out of business.

Withholding taxes fall under a special set of laws, and they are different from virtually all other kinds of taxes. That's because the money you withhold belongs to your employees, not to your company. In effect, you hold that money in trust for them until you turn it over to the government on their behalf. When your company doesn't make the payments, both civil and criminal penalties (including heavy fines and jail time) may apply.

The biggest penalty a company can incur for not remitting payroll taxes to the government is the 100 percent penalty (officially called the Trust Fund Recovery Penalty), and you can be held *personally liable* for paying it. If the IRS can prove that your company willfully didn't pay the taxes, you'll have to pay both the taxes *and* the penalty, which can be equal to the total taxes that were due. Willful nonpayment means that you chose not to pay the taxes, for whatever reason; and not paying them because your company doesn't have enough money counts as willful nonpayment.

UNEMPLOYMENT TAXES

When you have employees, chances are that you will be required to deal with the Federal Unemployment Tax (FUT), and possibly at least one state version of unemployment taxes as well. At the federal level, these taxes are paid only by employers (there's no withholding from employee pay here), and they're based directly on the total wages paid to employees. The FUT rate for 2016 was 6.0 percent, but that could be reduced if state unemployment insurance was also paid.

When it comes to state rules, though, there's a lot of variation. Here are the general rules of state unemployment taxes:

- They are generally paid by employers only
- They reduce the company's FUT burden
- The tax rate is based on how many employees have filed unemployment claims
- There's a cap on the maximum tax you'll owe for each employee

As you'd expect, the specifics vary pretty widely, especially when it comes to crunching the numbers. For example, the state unemployment insurance rate in Maryland in 2016 started at a standard rate of 2.6 percent, but the rate can vary from 0.3 to 7.5 percent, depending on the company's unemployment claims experience; the rate assigned to a company gets applied to the first $8,500 of earnings for each employee. So if an employee (in Maryland) earned $15,000, for example, your company would only owe unemployment taxes on the first $8,500 and not on the rest. In a couple of states, employees as well as employers have to pay in to the system (which adds extra withholding responsibilities for employers).

Overall, dealing with payroll and payroll taxes can be very time-consuming, and the rules are complex and change fairly frequently. For most business owners, the smart choice is to use a payroll company to handle all of these details—especially because the consequences of getting it wrong can be costly.

EARNING PROFITS, BUT OUT OF CASH

Too Much Month Left at the End of the Money

One of the most baffling accounting occurrences for new business owners is when their company shows a clear profit, but their cash is running frighteningly low. These startup entrepreneurs often confuse *making* money (meaning earning profits) with *having* money. Even strong profits don't always lead to sufficient cash, just as cash in the bank does not necessarily mean your business is clearing a healthy profit.

That sounds questionable, but it's true. Every time your company makes a sale on account, that sale indeed adds to your revenues and your profitability. But that on-account sale has absolutely no impact on your *cash* until the customer pays up. If you have a lot of slow-paying customers, that could put you into a big cash crunch. After all, even if your customers aren't paying, your company (and you) still has to pay the bills.

It's very common for new business owners to focus on sales, doing whatever they can to seal a deal. A lot of times that means extending credit to the customer, sometimes without making sure that the customer has a good payment record. Even customers with stellar credit history sometimes hit cash crunches of their own, and make late payments to keep their own cash flowing more smoothly. Payments that are late or never made can wreak havoc on your cash flow. Even though your sales numbers look great, and you're hitting all the sales goals you've set for the company, your company could still run out of cash.

Another place to look for "missing" cash is in prepaid expense accounts (which are asset accounts, not expense accounts). When your company makes a big lump prepayment to cover upcoming expenses, it hits your cash account and a prepaid asset account, without an equal match in an expense account. You might want to make a large prepayment in order to take advantage of savings (pay a year of rent up front to get one month free), or because it's a requirement (like an insurance policy). Either way, it drains current cash without having as large an impact on your profits, and therefore increases your tax bill (which you have to pay with cash).

Keep the Doors Open

About one in four businesses in the U.S. will fail because it has run out of cash (according to *Time*). And slightly more, about 29 percent of start-up businesses crash for the same reason. That's why religiously tracking your cash flow is more than just a good idea—it's the key to keeping the doors open.

FOLLOWING THE MONEY

The term "cash flow" describes the way money comes into and goes out of your business. As you might expect, when money comes in, it's called cash inflow; when money goes out, it's cash outflow. Keeping track of both sides of your cash equation is critical to the successful management of your company.

For many new and small businesses, the outflow will (at least initially) exceed the inflow, and that's called negative cash flow. Much better, of course, is the opposite situation, with more cash coming in than going out. That's the goal to strive for: positive cash flow. And if you have more money going out than coming in right now it doesn't necessarily mean that you are out of cash. If you have a sufficient cash cushion to get you through slow times, similar to a personal emergency savings account, a little imbalance won't cause a bankruptcy. However, you still need to work on establishing and maintaining a steady positive cash flow.

In order to successfully manage your cash flow, you need to know what's going on in your business right now, and what steps you can take to make the situation better. Start with a detailed cash flow projection, a sort of budget that tracks the cash moving into and out of your business. That will help you see where cash is going, and give you some ideas to stretch the outflow. In addition, you'll learn how cash comes in, and possibly find some ways to speed up that process. You have much more control over cash going out than you do over cash coming in, so that should be your initial cash management focus: minimizing cash shortfalls by keeping tighter reins on your cash outflow.

THE OPPOSITE HAPPENS, TOO

Your company can also be in a situation where it has plenty of cash, but it has negative income (net loss). This can happen when some expenses, like depreciation and amortization, have nothing to do with cash. Another reason could be that expenses you paid in advance (like prepaid rent or insurance) haven't yet been used up, so you're reaping those benefits without laying out additional cash. On top of that, if your company offers credit to customers, at some point you may have to write off some of those unpaid accounts as bad debt expense. These write offs will not impact your cash situation, but they do hit your bottom line.

The upside of this is that your company (and you) won't have to pay any income taxes when the period results in a net loss. That's another cash savings, and along with your positive cash balance, you'll have assets on hand to turn things around in the upcoming year.

Chapter 6
Financial Statements

To get a clear big-picture view of your company's financial position, you need three very special reports. These three reports are:

1. The statement of profit and loss
2. The balance sheet
3. The statement of cash flows

Virtually all small businesses prepare all three statements for every period. And that's good. But a lot of times the reports end up being filed away without so much as a glance—and that's a big mistake. Some business owners only look at their year-end numbers, some don't bother looking at them at all (figuring the accountant will point out any problems), and some give them just a quick glance before moving on to the next project. The most successful business owners use these statements to nip potential problems in the bud, to capitalize on surprising successes, and to make sure that the numbers are in line with what they expected. The best time to deal with any of these issues, even the good ones, is right away. And you can only do that when you take a careful look at what's going on.

In this chapter, you'll learn all you need to know about these statements, how they can help your business, and how these statements work together to offer the most complete picture of your company's financial strengths and weaknesses.

THE STATEMENT OF PROFIT AND LOSS

It's All about the Bottom Line

As a business owner, the statement of profit and loss might be your hands-down favorite because it shows you how much money your company is making. This statement can show you much more than the bottom line, though. It can let you know if you've been setting your prices too low, are paying too much for the merchandise that you resell, or are spending too much in delivery costs. In addition to spelling out just how well your business has done over the past year (or month or quarter), the statement of profit and loss contains clues for improving profitability and beefing up that bottom line.

Before you can see all that, though, you have to put the statement together, and accounting software makes doing that as easy as a single click or tap. Three kinds of accounts appear on this financial statement: revenues, costs, and expenses (all of which you learned about in the previous chapter). The statement is a kind of vertical equation that basically says "revenues minus costs minus expenses equals net profit (or loss)." This equation determines the look of the whole report.

HOW WILL IT LOOK?

The body of the statement of profit and loss report flows the exact same way as the equation, with revenues listed right on top; costs (if you sell products) coming next; and expenses located at the end. At the very bottom comes the bottom line, the company's overall net profit or loss for the period.

The Long and Short of It

Statements of profit and loss for service businesses are shorter than those for product-based businesses. Service companies don't need a section for cost of goods sold or gross profit, because they don't sell any goods. Other than that missing section, the statements look pretty much the same.

Most statements of profit and loss are topped with a standard report heading that contains three lines:

- The name of the company (ABC Company)
- The name of the statement (Statement of Profit and Loss)
- The time period covered by the statement (for the year ended December 31)

You have some leeway with the name of the statement, as long as readers can tell what kind of report it is. Other common names for this financial report include "income statement," "profit and loss statement," and "report of earnings." When your accountant talks about this report, she'll probably call it your P&L (that is, your profit and loss). Whatever name you use, the one thing that has to be spelled out specifically on this report is the time period line, which must reflect the actual fiscal period covered by the statement, whether it's a month, a quarter, or a year.

GETTING TO THE GROSS PROFIT

Gross profit is an important, and often overlooked, figure on the statement of profit and loss: It tells you in a single number whether you're charging enough for the products that you sell. Understanding gross profit, and knowing how to figure it out, are key steps in preparing this financial statement.

The statement of profit and loss is put together using data compiled from the actual business transactions that occurred during the fiscal period. It details how your company earned money, along with how much was spent in trying to create revenues. Once all of the raw revenue, cost, and expense numbers are available to determine gross profit, you put them together and start the calculations. Revenues always come first. Start with the gross revenues, which is really just another way of saying "total sales." If you have more than one sales account (such as one for products and another for services), you can list them individually and then total them, or just include the combined total figure. Then you subtract any contra sales accounts, such as sales discounts or sales returns. The result of that calculation is called your net sales. If you don't have any contra sales accounts, your gross sales and net sales will be the same, and you don't need to list both.

No Cash, No Sale

When your company uses the cash accounting method, only include sales for which the cash has already been received. If no cash has changed hands yet, don't include the sale. For accrual accounting, you have to include every sale transaction, regardless of whether your company has gotten any money.

For product-based businesses, the cost of goods sold section comes next. On your statement of profit and loss, you can either show the net cost of goods number or display the whole calculation. When you're doing the report for yourself, it's easier to have the calculation right there on the same page; when you're preparing the report for someone else, you may include just that final number in the financial statement along with a more detailed supporting schedule (which you would just attach to the back of the statement). The full-blown computation for cost of goods sold starts with your beginning inventory, and then adds in all the inventory purchases the company made during the period. The result gives you the total cost of goods available for sale. From that subtotal, subtract the ending inventory (what you have left in stock) to get the cost of goods sold. Next, subtract the cost of goods sold from the net sales to come up with your gross profit. This is the amount your company has left over to cover all of its operating expenses and also (hopefully) provide net profits.

For service businesses, that cost of goods section doesn't apply, meaning the net sales number is really the same as the gross profit. Whichever type of business you have, getting to the gross profit gives you very important information: It lets you know what you have left to cover all of the company's expenses, hopefully with something left over for a positive bottom line result.

GETTING TO THE BOTTOM LINE

The next section of the statement of profit and loss is common to all businesses, whether they sell products or not, and it includes all of the company's expenses for the period. You can choose to group the expenses—into variable and fixed, or sales and general, for example—or you can just list them all in one big group. The most common division of groups is selling expenses, and general and administrative expenses. If you don't have a lot of different expense accounts, though, it's easier for you to just keep them all together. Regardless of how or whether you divide up your expenses on the report, you still need to come to a grand total for all of the operating expenses.

Now that you know how to calculate your gross profit and tally your operating expenses, you're ready to calculate your company's bottom line. To get to the profit or loss for the period, subtract the total operating expenses from the gross profit (which equals revenues minus costs, for product-based businesses) or from the net sales (for service businesses). When the result is positive, your company has made a profit for the period; when the result is negative, it has sustained a loss for the period.

THE BALANCE SHEET

Finances Frozen in Time

A balance sheet provides a financial snapshot of your business, frozen at a particular point in time. Also known as the statement of financial position, this report gives you a comprehensive picture of where your business stands. The balance sheet contains current pictures of your assets, liabilities, and equity. Looking at it lets you see what your company has and how much it owes, and it reveals your updated equity share.

HOW WILL IT LOOK?

Balance sheets are usually prepared in a standard format to make it easier for people to compare different periods for a single company (usually for the business owners) or different companies in the same period (something potential investors or lenders might want to see). For business owners, this comparability between periods offers a glimpse of progress at a glance; for potential investors or lenders, the ability to compare apples to apples offers better information for making decisions.

There are two commonly used options for a standard balance sheet layout:

- Vertical
- Side-by-side

In the vertical format, the three categories are listed one after the other; assets come first, followed by liabilities, and finally equity. In the side-by-side format, assets appear on the left side of the statement, and liabilities and equity are located on the right. How you decide to lay it out is really a matter of personal preference. But no matter how your balance sheet is laid out, the report will always include the three permanent account categories:

1. Assets
2. Liabilities
3. Owner's equity

Your balance sheet also follows the rule of the accounting equation: assets must equal liabilities plus owner's equity (with accounting software, it's virtually impossible for the accounts to be out of balance).

It's a Snapshot

Of all the financial statements, the balance sheet is the only one that comes with a specific date rather than an activity period. That's because it tells you the balance of your permanent accounts on a fixed day—most commonly the last day of an accounting period.

While this looks simple so far, your balance sheet will contain more than three key numbers. Remember, individual assets and liabilities fall into different categories. Those categories appear as sections on the balance sheet, and accounts are listed in their associated categories. Following this organizational pattern makes it easier to do a quick analysis of your balance sheet at a glance. Let's take a look at how you'll put this statement together.

ASSET CATEGORIES

On the balance sheet, a company's assets will be broken out into the four basic categories (or fewer, if the company doesn't have assets in a given category) of assets that we discussed in Chapter 4, and listed in this order:

- **Current assets:** Current assets include anything that's *expected* to be converted into cash within a year of the balance sheet date. On the balance sheet, these assets are listed in order of liquidity. The assets that can be turned into cash the fastest are listed first.
- **Long-term investments:** Long-term investments are regular investments that your company owns as a way to generate extra income over the long haul. These investments can be stocks, bonds, or mutual funds, or even land that the company is holding on to for investment purposes.
- **Fixed assets:** Common fixed assets owned by the majority of businesses include things like office furniture and equipment, computer systems, vehicles, and shop displays. If your company has fixed assets on the balance sheet, it will also have accumulated depreciation, which is recorded in the fixed-asset contra account that holds all of the depreciation expense that's been accounted for so far.
- **Intangible (or other) assets:** Intangible assets include things such as patents and trademarks, which have plenty of value but no real physical form. Their decline in value is measured over time as amortization expense (quite similar to depreciation expense), but there's usually no separate accumulated amortization contra account. Instead, for accounting purposes, the asset account gets decreased directly as it loses value over time.

Most new and small businesses will find the bulk of their assets in the current and fixed categories, so the asset section of their balance sheets will be brief.

LIABILITY CATEGORIES

As you learned in Chapter 4, liabilities come in two basic flavors: current and long-term. Here, we'll look at how liability accounts appear on the balance sheet.

Current liabilities include any debts or obligations that will come due within one year of the balance sheet date, mainly the day-to-day stuff, such as accounts payable and sales tax payable (you'll notice that current liabilities have the word "payable" as part of their names). Current liabilities may also include accrued expenses (like taxes or wages, expenses incurred but not yet paid) for companies that use the accrual accounting method.

Long-term liabilities are debts and obligations that will be outstanding for more than one year; however, the part of a long-term liability that is due in the upcoming 12 months is usually put in the current category. Such long-term liabilities typically include loans, such as business startup loans or mortgages.

OWNER'S EQUITY

The final piece of the balance sheet is the owner's equity, and its layout depends on the business entity. Sole proprietorships, partnerships, and most LLCs will have owner's capital accounts. Corporations will have a combination of shareholder's equity and retained earnings. Whichever form it takes, the owner's equity reflects the net worth of the company.

THE STATEMENT OF CASH FLOWS

Where Did All the Money Go?

Statements of cash flows are the most complicated of the standard financial reports prepared at the end of every accounting period. But accounting software makes their creation, at least, a snap. This statement tracks a company's cash movement, and it's the most critical report for keeping your new business afloat. If you do decide to give it a go and create this report manually (try it at least once, for the experience), the ending cash balance will tell you immediately whether you've done it right or not. Simply, the ending cash balance has to equal the current cash number.

WHAT DOES IT COVER?

The statement of cash flows covers the same time period as the statement of profit and loss. For example, if the statement of profit and loss covers one month, then the statement of cash flows must also cover this same one-month span. The statement of cash flows starts with the beginning cash balance for the period (which is the same as the ending cash balance for the last period). Then, there are three categories (formatted on the report into separate sections) that track the way cash flows in and out of your company:

- Operating activities
- Investing activities
- Financing activities

The operating activities section includes all the regular daily transactions that bring in or use up cash. Mainly, these will be revenues and expenses. The investing activities section includes buying and selling long-term assets that are used by the company. These assets may include things such as stocks and bonds, as well as fixed assets and property improvements (for example, paying to have a building renovated). The financing activities section includes the things you do to raise cash for your company. These activities might include taking out loans or bringing in more equity contributions; it would also include the payments you make as you pay down debt or pay out dividends.

WHY THE CASH SOURCE MATTERS

Of the three sections detailing your company's cash flows, operating activities is the most important. This category speaks to how successfully your business maintains a positive cash position solely through its daily transactions. If your company is generating enough cash to survive from its operating activities, its chances of staying afloat and flourishing are very good.

However, if your company can bring cash in only by selling off assets, taking on debt, or tapping into your personal funds, then the company's future might be in doubt. None of these are long-term solutions. If you sell off all of your assets, they can't work as income-producers for you. Debt has to be repaid, on time and with interest, or you could find yourself in bankruptcy court. And while debt can be refinanced, taking on additional new debt for the sole purpose of paying off existing debt is a dangerous cycle to start. Finally, you started a business in the hopes of creating wealth for yourself and your family; draining your personal cash to fund a floundering business won't achieve that goal.

Perhaps the Most Important for Investors

Investors looking at a corporation's financial statements often skip the cash flows, but that may be the most important statement of all. If a company is hemorrhaging cash in its operating activities, and borrowing funds to pick up the slack, its chances of staying afloat are pretty slim and it's a good time to sell off the investment.

HOW WILL IT LOOK?

You can use either of two different formats to prepare your statement of cash flows: direct or indirect. Of the two, the indirect format is simpler to prepare, and is much more popular for that reason. The format difference really appears only in the operating activities section; the other sections look the same either way.

The Direct Method

The direct method focuses on grouping the major sources of cash receipts and causes of cash payments. For example, cash used to pay for inventory is listed separately from cash used to pay employees. The cash coming in and the cash going out are summed to come up with the total cash provided (or used, if it's negative) by operating activities. This can get complicated for companies using the accrual accounting method, which may not separate cash and non-cash transactions. For example, all sales would be recorded in the sales account whether they were cash or on-account sales. Because cash transactions appear on this statement, companies who want to use the direct method may have to alter they way they record and track transactions.

The Indirect Method

The indirect method starts with your net income (or net loss) for the period and converts it into cash flow. For example, noncash expenses such as depreciation are added back to the bottom-line number, and accruals and deferrals (used in accrual basis accounting) are converted into their cash effect. Here's how a conversion works: A decrease in accounts receivable from the period prior to this one indicates more cash has come in, since accounts receivable decreases based on customer payments. That converts on-account sales information into the cash effect for this period. The basic conversion strategy is this: Increases in assets, such as accounts receivable, translate to decreases in cash, and vice versa; increases in liabilities, such as accounts payable, translate to increases in cash, and vice versa.

Whichever statement style you choose, the results will be the same. Either style will clearly trace the movement of cash in and out of your business. Most accounting software programs will let you choose the style you prefer, and switch back and forth between them.

WHAT FINANCIAL STATEMENTS TELL YOU

Read Between the Number Lines

Now that you know how to prepare these important financial statements, let's take a look at what they can tell you. Financial statements contain a wealth of information; you just need to know where to look. More than just a yardstick for past performance, your financial statements can provide significant clues for maximizing profitability, improving cash flow, and successfully growing your business. They'll help you make decisions, large and small, and maybe even point your company in directions you never dreamed of. Whether your business is brand new or several years old, there's a lot to be learned from your financial statements, and now is the time to get started.

In addition to creating these statements for yourself, you may have to put them together for someone else to review. For example, the statement of profit and loss will show up on your company's tax return. When you have a bank loan, the bank may want to monitor your balance sheet.

Then there's the investor's perspective. If you're considering investing your hard-earned money in the stock market, check out the financial statements of any corporation that might make its way into your portfolio. The same information, presented in basically the same way, appears on every set of financial statements, whether they're revealing the results of your small company's first year in business or the financial performance of a *Fortune* 500 corporation.

WHAT CAN YOUR COMPANY'S STATEMENTS TELL YOU?

At face value, your financial statements tell you a lot about your company's performance. The statement of profit and loss lets you know how much the company sold, and whether those sales resulted in overall profitability. The balance sheet tells you where the company stands right now, and gives you a look at the overall financial position. The statement of cash flows informs you of how cash moves through your business, and whether operations are supplying or draining cash. All of this data is critical to your future plans, but it's really just a small part of the total knowledge you can gain from these exceptionally enlightening reports.

When you delve deeper into these statements, and add a little math to the mix, you will open up a whole new world of information that you can use to make your business a better one. With critical analysis, the relationships among the accounts become clearer, as does the impact they can have on one another. Different ways of measuring the same numbers offer new perspectives and insights, and can spark innovative and profitable ideas. Your financial statements can tell you things such as:

- Whether your company has sufficient liquidity
- Whether the company is holding too much inventory
- Whether you need to revisit customer payment terms
- Whether you're charging enough for your products and services
- How to put your assets to better use
- When it's safe to take on some debt
- Whether serious financial problems are on the horizon
- How well your company stacks up to competitors

- How well the company fares according to industry standards
- Whether your company is ready to grow

The more you know about your business, the better its chances of success. Noticing potential problem areas before they blossom into full-grown crises can save a business from ultimate failure. Planning and allowing for growth before it kicks in helps your company expand in the most profitable ways. Your financial statements contain all of this information; all you have to do is analyze it.

WORKING CAPITAL MEASURES FINANCIAL HEALTH

You can tell a lot about a company's current financial well-being by looking at its working capital. This simple balance sheet calculation lets you see how efficiently a company is using its resources. To calculate working capital, you subtract current liabilities from current assets:

current assets – current liabilities = working capital

Why is this so important? Because if a company's current liabilities exceed its current assets, the company may not be able to pay its bills, at least in the short term. In the most extreme cases, negative working capital can end in bankruptcy, or the dissolution of the business. In addition, working capital gives an indication of how efficiently the company is operating. If the working capital figure is very high, it could indicate that the company has too much inventory (or slow-moving inventory) on hand, or that its accounts receivable customers aren't paying their bills promptly. Assets tied up as inventory or accounts receivable are still current assets, but they can't be used to pay the bills.

To see at a glance where the working capital of your company (or a company you're thinking about investing in) falls on the scale, calculate the working capital ratio, which is simply total current assets divided by total current liabilities. A healthy working capital ratio generally falls between 1.2 and 3.0, depending on the size of the business and the industry it's in. If the working capital ratio is below 1.0, it means the company has negative working capital, and may not be able to pay its current bills on time. The working capital ratio may also be called the current ratio.

A LITTLE MORE MATH
CAN REVEAL A LOT

In addition to knowing the working capital and the working capital (or current) ratio, there are a couple more ratios that can let you know how a company is faring.

The Quick Ratio

The quick ratio is similar to the current ratio, but leaves inventory out of the calculation. Computing the quick ratio can give you a more honest assessment of a company's ability to pay its current bills. Here's how you calculate the quick ratio:

(current assets – inventory) ÷ current liabilities

The reason some business gurus recommend focusing on this ratio is because inventory can't always be counted on to bring in as much cash as was laid out to buy it. For example, if your shop needs to clear out bathing suits to make room for winter coats, you might sell those lingering bathing suits at deep discounts—even below your cost—just to get rid of them. Plus, inventory doesn't always sell as quickly as you'd like it to.

The Debt to Equity Ratio

Another good measure of a company's solvency—this time over the long haul—is its debt to equity ratio. Here's how you figure out the debt to equity ratio for a business:

total liabilities ÷ total equity

This calculation lets you know exactly how dependent a company is on debt to survive. If debt outweighs equity (which means ownership), that could indicate financial trouble on the horizon. For that reason, a lower number is more favorable than a higher number.

What's the Equity?

The equity accounts that appear on your balance sheet depend on the business structure. If your company is a proprietorship or a partnership, there will be a capital account for each owner. If it's a corporation, the shareholder's equity will include at least common stock (or shares) and retained earnings.

FINANCIAL STATEMENTS FROM AN INVESTOR'S PERSPECTIVE

Before you invest even $1 in a corporation's stock, take a good look at its most recent financial statements (preferably for the last few years). The same information you would use to assess your own company's health and potential can tell you a lot about a prospective investment. While you can find this information in the company's slickly packaged annual report, to cut through the propaganda and hyperbole go straight to the audited financial statements they're required to file with the SEC (Securities and Exchange Commission).

On its website (www.sec.gov), the SEC has an online comprehensive database called EDGAR (Electronic Data Gathering, Analysis, and Retrieval) that holds every corporate filing submitted to the agency—more than 20 million documents. There, the annual audited financial statements are included in a filing called the 10-K. EDGAR gives individual investors access to the same information at the same time as massive institutional investors.

Pay Attention to the Footnotes

There's a saying among financial professionals: Accountants hide the problems in the footnotes. Problems are hidden there because financial statement footnotes are a lot like fine print; most of us don't have the stomach to read all the way through it. Some companies use that to their advantage.

That sounds fishy, but it isn't. In fact, it's perfectly legal and extremely common for that kind of information to be disclosed in the corporation's financial statement footnotes. And even when a company has nothing to hide, the footnotes can offer deeper insights into the company's current operations and future plans—and that's information investors need to know. The footnotes explain all numbers found in the financial statements, spelling out how they were calculated and detailing explanations of the results.

In the first section of the footnotes (the explanatory information for the financial statements) you'll find the specifics of the corporation's accounting practices, including which valuation methods they've used and when they recognize revenue, a critical part of the company's earnings. To assess whether or not their choices make sense, you can look into what the industry standard is to see whether this company is following it. If it's not, and the corporation you're thinking of buying into is using a more aggressive accounting method, then it could be a red flag that the company is trying to hide negative performance or use an accounting trick to make the results seem better than they were.

The next section of the footnotes typically includes detailed disclosures, mainly information the company must provide that doesn't quite fit neatly into the financial statements. Some information you might find here would be details about:

- Error corrections
- Accounting adjustments
- Changes in accounting procedures
- Long-term debt
- ESOPs (employee stock ownership plans)
- Outstanding stock options
- Ongoing or upcoming legal battles

Keep in mind that the language in financial statement footnotes is often full of legal jargon, making it very challenging to slog through. Though it's not always the case, lengthy paragraphs and complex language can be used to conceal things the corporation doesn't want investors to read about. In a now classic example, Enron actually disclosed most of their misdeeds in the footnotes to their financial statements, but practically no one read them.

FINANCIAL STATEMENTS FLOW INTO TAX RETURNS

The IRS Wants to Know Everything

One of the biggest uses for all the accounting work you've done throughout the year is to prepare the company's tax return. No matter what industry your business is in, the tax return depends mainly on the business structure (sole proprietorship, partnership, LLC, or corporation). Your company has to file a business tax return every year, whether your business earned profits or sustained a loss. Only profits lead to income taxes, though, and that's a pretty good problem to have.

That's actually one of the reasons financial statements were created in the first place: to satisfy tax collectors. Without the financial statements, neither you nor the tax authority would have any idea if your company was earning profits, the value of its assets, or what kind of equity structure was in place. All of this information flows from the financial statements right into tax returns.

TAX RETURN OR FINANCIAL STATEMENT?

The first time you look at any business tax return form—from a Schedule C for sole proprietors (which usually includes freelancers and consultants) to Form 1120 for a C corporation—you'll notice that it resembles your company's financial statements, just without the numbers filled in yet. That's really all the tax return is, after all: a standard form on which to report your company's revenues, costs, expenses, and net profit or loss. Some business tax returns also ask for balance sheet information; again, the form looks just like an empty balance sheet, and you just have to fill in the blanks.

The biggest difference between your financial statements and your tax return is the layout. For tax purposes, you combine different numbers than you would for your own review or planning purposes. For example, there's a single line for tax expenses on some business tax returns. There you would lump together payroll taxes, property taxes, and any other non-income-based taxes. On your own statement of profit and loss, though, you list those very different taxes separately. The order of items on the tax return probably won't exactly match your financial statements, either. But every revenue, cost, and expense you've recorded throughout the year will show up on the tax return, in one form or another.

The same goes for tax returns that include pared-down balance sheets (for some corporations and partnerships). For tax returns, all of your asset, liability, and equity account balances need to be included (or the report won't balance), but these items will not necessarily appear in the same way they do on your balance sheet.

IF THE COMPANY DOESN'T PAY TAXES, WHY DOES IT FILE A RETURN?

That's a very common question among new small business owners, because many of these companies don't actually pay any income taxes themselves. Except for C corporations (and limited liability companies that choose to be treated like C corporations), all other businesses are what accountants refer to as pass-through entities. Unlike the others, C corporations are subject to income tax

The Double Taxation Conundrum

With C corporations, profits get taxed twice. First, the corporation pays income tax on its profits for the year. Then, shareholders have to pay tax on any distributed profits, or dividends. If you own a C corporation and you take out some of the profits, you've just earned taxable dividends.

Partnerships and (most) LLCs must complete and file Form 1065. From there, each partner or LLC member gets a Form K-1 that details his share of the company's revenues, costs, expenses, and profits (or losses). S corporations file Form 1120-S, again kicking out Forms K-1 for the owners.

HOW THESE STATEMENTS INTERCONNECT

This Number Goes Over There Now

Even though they each contain very distinct information, the three main financial statements are completely connected. In fact, you can't produce a balance sheet without first creating a statement of profit and loss, and you can't prepare a statement of cash flows without having already produced the other two financial statements.

A Look Backward

No matter which statement you're working with, all of the numbers will be pulled from the general ledger (except the numbers that are determined from the calculations on the statements themselves). All of these statements also speak to the past; they are reporting what happened during the prior period, rather than what's to come.

The statement of profit and loss contains the bottom-line earnings for the period, whether they're positive (for profits) or negative (for losses). Those earnings are folded into the owner's equity, on the balance sheet, at the end of the period. Without that step, the balance sheet could not balance; the equity accounts are not complete until they reflect the current period earnings.

The balance sheet is sort of the financial statement middleman. It pulls information from the statement of profit and loss, and offers information to the statement of cash flows. As you might guess, the statement of cash flows needs to know how much cash the company started the period with, and then works down to the ending cash balance. Sometimes, it needs additional balance sheet information as well, such as the changes in accounts receivable and accounts payable. The statement of cash flows also gives something back to the balance sheet: verification. If the ending cash on the balance sheet doesn't match the ending cash on the statement of cash flows, there's a mistake somewhere that needs to be fixed.

The statement of cash flows also pulls information off of the statement of profit and loss. Revenues generate cash, even if it's not immediate (as in the case of credit sales). Costs and expenses eat up cash, though again, the impact may not be immediately apparent.

REVENUES AND EXPENSES ON THE BALANCE SHEET

Revenue, cost, and expense accounts don't directly appear on the balance sheet, but they do affect balance sheet accounts with virtually every transaction that includes them. A company can't make a single sale, pay even one expense, or calculate costs without involving an asset or liability account; and, in the end, the net result of revenues, costs, and expenses will make a change in the company's equity.

When a company makes a sale, it hits either the cash or accounts receivable account. If that sale involved a product, inventory comes into play. Paying for rent, insurance, office supplies, and electricity increases the company's expenses, and those payments also hit either cash or accounts payable.

So you can see that even before the net income (or loss) for the fiscal period gets rolled up into equity, every revenue, cost, and expense transaction hits the balance sheet in one way or another . . . and that goes both ways.

ASSETS AND LIABILITIES HIT THE STATEMENT OF PROFIT AND LOSS

You've just seen how revenues and expenses have an everyday effect on the balance sheet. Now we'll take a look at how changes in the balance sheet can affect the statement of profit and loss.

Every fixed asset a company owns is subject to depreciation—an expense. The same holds true for intangible assets and amortization expense. Those expenses, brought on by assets, make a quick U-turn and head back to the balance sheet as accumulated depreciation and accumulated amortization (or as a direct reduction of the intangible asset balance).

Long-term liabilities can also activate accounts on the statement of profit and loss. For example, notes payable (like mortgages or shareholder loans) and bonds payable generate interest expense.

EVERYTHING IMPACTS CASH FLOW

One way or another, every balance sheet account, and every revenue, cost, or expense that turns up on the statement of profit and loss affects (or will eventually affect) cash. Purchasing assets reduces cash, through down payments or loan payments. Paying down liabilities reduces cash. Owner withdrawals and dividend payouts decrease cash. Sales increase cash; costs and expenses eat up cash. Other than wholly non-cash transactions like recording depreciation expense, or converting inventory into cost of goods sold, all transactions lead back to cash in some way, at some point.

As you can see, recording transactions, preparing financial statements, and analyzing the results can be time-consuming and labor-intensive, but it's all critical to the accounting process. Thankfully, we no longer have to do all of this by hand, as evolving software handles more accounting procedures every year.

Chapter 7
Accounting Moves Forward

So now that you know the ins and outs of accounting it's time to consider what the future has in store for the accounting industry. Where the industry moves next depends largely on political, social, and economic changes. What we know for sure is this: Accountants will adapt and expand their skills to reflect whatever people and businesses need. No doubt, technology advances will cause some traditional accounting tasks to fade into the background and set the stage for new directions and capabilities.

But before accountants leap into the future, they must still understand what's come before, which we'll take a look at in this chapter. Historical events—stock market crashes, bank failures, recessions, epidemic fraud, and more—play a big role in shaping the rules and regulations that guide the profession.

No matter what happens tomorrow, though, there's always one thing accountants can bank on: debits on the left, credits on the right.

THE BIG ACCOUNTING FIRMS

And Then There Were Four

Back in the 1970s, eight large national accounting firms emerged. They were called the Big Eight, and they brought in the most revenue in the industry. The most successful, prestigious corporations hired these firms to audit their financial statements, and investors and regulators alike fully trusted the integrity of the accountants at these firms. The names of these Big Eight firms may be familiar (some for notorious reasons):

1. Deloitte Haskins & Sells
2. Touche, Ross & Co.
3. Arthur Andersen & Co.
4. Arthur Young & Co.
5. Price Waterhouse
6. Coopers & Lybrand
7. Ernst & Whinney
8. Peat, Marwick, Mitchell & Co.

The year 1989 saw two enormous mergers, bringing the total to a Big Six. Deloitte Haskins & Sells joined with Touche, Ross to form Deloitte & Touche; and Arthur Young & Co. merged with Ernst & Whinney to create Ernst & Young. Nine years later, in 1998, Price Waterhouse combined with Coopers & Lybrand, resulting in PricewaterhouseCoopers.

Scandal brought the new total to a Big Four in 2002 when Arthur Andersen closed its doors on the heels of the Enron debacle. And while the degree of trust in these mega-accounting firms isn't what it once was, the Big Four still carry the most prestige and power in the industry.

PWC RAKES IN TOP DOLLARS

In terms of revenue, PwC (as PricewaterhouseCoopers is now known) leads the Big Four pack. This accounting powerhouse firm has more than 208,000 professional employees serving in 157 countries and its current revenues top $35.4 billion.

PwC remains firmly fixed in traditional accounting services, particularly audits, snagging 29 percent of the audit work for the *Fortune* Global 500, along with 56 percent of that illustrious group for other services. Clients of the accounting giant have included Goodyear, ExxonMobil, and Bank of America.

DELOITTE US SHIFTS GEARS

Now part of the multinational firm Deloitte Touche Tohmatsu Limited (DTTL), which is headquartered in the United Kingdom, Deloitte US serves the vast majority of *Fortune* 500 companies. To get the job done, Deloitte employs more than 225,000 professionals across 150 countries. They bring in around $35.2 billion a year.

Although Deloitte US offers accounting, auditing, and tax services, their focus has shifted toward business consulting and advisory services.

EY IS GROWING FAST

EY was known as Ernst & Young until 2013, and along with the name change, their core philosophy changed as well, redefining the firm's purpose as "Building a better working world." Though it's not the biggest of the Big Four, EY has been the fastest growing in terms of both revenues and employees. In 2015, their workforce grew by 12.3 percent to 211,450 employees worldwide; and their revenues also grew by 12 percent that year, to more than $28 billion.

Along with traditional accounting services, EY now specializes in areas like climate change and sustainability, global business networks, and growth markets. The firm is also known for its diverse staff and commitment to minimizing its global footprint.

KPMG HITS BIG

Back in 1987, Peat Marwick International merged with Klynveld Main Goerdeler (KMG) to form KPMG (Klynveld Peat Marwick Goerdeler), which created the largest accounting firm in the world (at the time). The union married Peat Marwick's North American foothold with KMG's European base to solidify a position in the growing international financial marketplace.

With nearly 174,000 employees worldwide, KPMG serves 155 countries. The firm's revenues hit $24.4 billion in 2015, cementing its place in the Big Four. Among their more high profile clients, KPMG has done accounting work for the U.S. Department of Homeland Security, Burger King, and General Electric.

SCANDALS IN THE ACCOUNTING WORLD

The Fix Is In

Whenever there's money on the line, swindles and scandals can rear their ugly heads. White collar crimes, like embezzlement and corporate fraud, are alarmingly commonplace. Sadly, greed and corruption impact even the professionals we're supposed to be able to place our highest trust in: CPAs.

Often, huge financial scandals (like the big bank failures in 2008 and a tidal wave of fraud hitting in the early 2000s) result in new legislation and tighter scrutiny. Changes like these can improve corporate responsibility and provide better guidance for the millions of ethical accountants out there.

Let's take a look at some of the more notorious accounting scandals and some of the legislation they helped inspire.

THE ENRON TIDAL WAVE

Before everything hit the fan in 2001, the public was led to believe that Enron was one of the most successful companies in the United States. As it turned out, the company had fooled regulators and investors alike with an elaborate accounting scheme that kept hundreds of millions of dollars' worth of debt off the balance sheet, hidden from plain view.

On top of that, corporate execs also fiddled with revenues by creating shell companies (an inactive company set up for the purpose of financial maneuvering) they could use to inflate their income. The company's earnings were greatly inflated, but that didn't raise any alarm bells for the CPA firm auditing Enron. In fact, Arthur Andersen (their accounting firm) never even reported a problem, and just kept signing off on the corporation's fraudulent financial statements. When Enron hit rock bottom and declared bankruptcy in 2001, thousands of employees lost their jobs, and millions of investors saw their holdings plummet in value.

Too Small to Embezzle?

Embezzlement covers everything from corporate executives who turn in million-dollar expense reports to sales clerks who pocket $10 at the register. Any time someone breaks the trust placed in him to monitor assets, and takes those assets for himself, he's an embezzler.

THE BACKDATED OPTIONS SCAM

A wave of scandal hit the corporate world in the mid-2000s, leading to more than 50 resignations of top executives at companies all across the United States. Many big-name companies were painted with that scandal brush, including:

- Cheesecake Factory
- Staples
- UnitedHealth Group
- Apple
- And many others

The story really starts back in the 1970s, when a new accounting rule let corporations pay their executives with "at-the-money" stock options (meaning the options were granted at that day's market price) without having to record any salary expense. Basically, they could pay their executives more money without taking a hit to the bottom line, though they'd still get a deduction for tax purposes.

Some unscrupulous executives realized they could fiddle with the options by picking a past date when the stock was trading for a very low price, then backdating their options. For example, if a CEO got stock options on May 1 when the stock was trading for $50 per share, $50 would be his option price, and he'd have to wait for the stock price to increase before he could profit. But if he backdated the options to March 10, when shares were trading for just $44 each, he would profit right away. With those backdated options, he could buy the stock for $44 per share on May 1, and sell them for the current trading price of $50, earning a $6 profit on every single share.

After a Pulitzer Prize–winning exposé in the *Wall Street Journal* and an intense SEC (Securities and Exchange Commission) investigation, the backdating executives resigned in shame, and the accounting rules were changed. To combat this fraud, corporations now have to report any stock options they grant within two days.

GLOBAL AND LOCAL CORPORATIONS MAKE SCANDALOUS HEADLINES

Over the past few years, we've seen the enormous impact of corporate fraud, and not just the way it affects the financial markets. Some have been large, others small, but they all undermine faith in the reliability of financial statements and corporate governance. Here's a look at a few of the big ones:

- In 2016, three former executives of Tesco (a British supermarket chain) were charged with criminal fraud linked to a $420 million accounting scandal uncovered in 2014.
- Investigators are still looking into the Valeant Pharmaceuticals accounting racket that involved, among other things, a secret corporate relationship, inventory shifting, and fraudulent insurance claims.
- The Volkswagen scandal led to millions of cars being recalled, along with a giant dip in the corporation's stock price, and a $20 billion loss of market capitalization.

Corporate fraud still happens with alarming frequency, and CPAs and forensic accountants work overtime to limit the occurrences and their impact. But rapidly changing economies and increasing international business ties can make tracking tricky, and vastly different regulations in different countries confuse the issue even more. That's why the accounting profession is constantly evolving—to meet tomorrow's challenges.

BIG CHANGES IN THE INDUSTRY

From the Abacus to the App

Like everything else in the world, the accounting industry has been fundamentally changed by advances in technology. The days of summing long columns of numbers, painstakingly ensuring everything balances, and manually creating financial reports are long gone; all of those tasks are automated now. Without the grind of number crunching, which used to fill up long days hunched over adding machines, accounting professionals have been able to reimagine their careers, and activate the more creative side of their brains.

On top of that, the advent of cloud computing and mobile financial apps has allowed people, including business owners, to take a more active role in accounting and bookkeeping. Now, instead of having their accountants prepare journal entries and create financial statements, people are calling on these seasoned financial professionals for other skills: advice and guidance, business and tax planning, and refined specialties that involve things like technology and forensics. Let's take a look at some of the most recent changes.

SHRINKING HARDWARE CHANGES SOFTWARE

Today, all you need to create a personal budget, prepare company financial statements, or track your investment portfolio is a smartphone and a couple of apps. Sure, multinational corporations still have IT (information technology) departments, server rooms, teams of accountants and accounting staff, and (more often than not) proprietary accounting software. But technology and the economy are shifting, and accounting software is changing with it.

With billions of people using smartphones and tablets instead of laptops or desktop computers, software development has focused more on apps and cloud computing. Instead of downloading programs, or installing them via CD, people are turning to online software solutions—particularly the ones that go mobile. While you can't carry your company's computer system around with you, you can carry a smartphone that fits right in your pocket and use it to gain instant access to the accounting and financial information you need, wherever you are.

This mobile technology also gives accountants instant, up-to-the-minute access to the books of their clients. Instead of spending nine days in a client's conference room, poring over handwritten records and receipts, compiling dozens of journal entries, accountants can now simply connect with their clients on the cloud to review tricky transactions as they're made. They can pick up and analyze client finances without ever leaving their offices, or they can do it from the coffee shop downstairs. Client-prepared financial statements can be easily reviewed, quickly adjusted (for error corrections or to comply with GAAP requirements), and seamlessly dropped into payroll, sales, and income tax returns—and it can all be done on a smartphone or tablet.

MORE CLIENT DIY

Of course, as software and apps make basic accounting and bookkeeping tasks as easy as eating pizza, more people than ever are doing this work themselves. Online banking, credit card, and brokerage accounts can link seamlessly into most any accounting or tax software. That automation eliminates the common math errors and missed transactions that used to plague bookkeepers and accountants alike. People no longer need to rely on accountants and bookkeepers to deal with their business transactions, or even to do their taxes. Now, everything is DIY, and more often than not, accounting work is done in the cloud.

No More Mistaeks

Since electronic spreadsheet programs came into use decades ago, many common math errors have become virtually extinct . . . except for one. Software can't recognize a transposition input error, like typing in $160 instead of $610, if it doesn't knock anything out of balance, but a seasoned accountant can and will notice the error.

And as clients do more of the work for themselves, and computers pick up the rest of the mathematical grunt work, the roles and responsibilities of accountants continue to change.

CYBERSECURITY TAKES CENTER STAGE

As accounting data moves to the Internet, CPAs and their clients must step up their cybersecurity efforts. Global criminal cabals hack and attack vulnerable networks, trawling for sensitive financial information, social security numbers, and corporate secrets.

Clients trust their CPAs with their most sensitive information, and those accountants are charged with doing everything possible to keep that data safeguarded. That protection has to start right on the front lines, with the accountants themselves. It's crucial that these trusted professionals be cyberfraud savvy: never clicking on links in phishing emails, immediately reporting even suspected security issues, using caution and respecting confidentiality on social media sites, using extreme caution when sending information by email, and being constantly vigilant for viruses and system incursions.

Security awareness is an ongoing issue: You can't just install a firewall and some antivirus software and hope that it's enough to keep out hackers and identity thieves. System security measures must be reviewed regularly and updated frequently. For example, accountants must make sure to use the strongest possible encryption and passwords for information stored in the cloud, and change those passwords regularly. They must also limit access to client information to only the professionals who are working on that account, and they must encrypt sensitive information sent by email with password-protected documents, and then communicate the password separately. These kinds of steps are crucial for protecting client (and personal) financial information.

ACCOUNTING SOFTWARE

Fast, Easy, Accurate

Today, the adding machine has gone the way of the abacus and is now used only as a decoration or as part of a museum exhibit. This long-time staple of the accounting profession is no longer necessary now that computers have taken over the more mundane tasks of accounting.

Computerizing accounting entries saves you time and provides a variety of other concrete benefits. These benefits include the elimination of calculation errors that in turn minimizes the time needed to hunt for mistakes. In addition, these technologies offer immediate analysis and reporting on demand, supplying instant information for decision-making.

Today we have online software, on-the-go financial apps, and technologies that the first accountants could never have imagined. Still, many accountants hold on to the basics, and continue to use the first digital technological innovation that took the industry by storm: the electronic spreadsheet. Here you'll learn all you need to know about this innovation, along with some information on what type of software to buy, what type of advanced accounting systems you need (if any), and what to do with tax software. Let's take a look!

ROWS AND COLUMNS

The first steps toward more automated accounting came in the form of electronic spreadsheets that could be used on personal computers. Before that, spreadsheets were done by hand, on paper, which took enormous amounts of time. With the advent of mainframe computing in the mid-twentieth century, accountants could enter that information into a computer—if they were lucky enough to have access to such a system—but they couldn't really see what they were doing until the data was compiled and spit back out. This first step represented a breakthrough innovation to be sure, but the real revolution was yet to come.

VisiCalc and Lotus 1-2-3

As so often happens, necessity changed the face of electronic spreadsheets. Thanks to a Harvard MBA student named Dan Bricklin who had a then visionary idea, the type of spreadsheets we use today was born. Bricklin was working on a case study and realized he had to either do a lot of writing or find a timeshare spot on the mainframe (literally signing up to get a time slot of access to the computer). Neither of those ideas appealed to him, which sparked the idea for what would become VisiCalc, the first computer-based spreadsheet where you could see what you were doing as you did it, and manipulate the numbers on the fly, all on a personal computer.

VisiCalc was designed for early Apple computers. As IBM PCs came into fashion, another more robust spreadsheet program called Lotus 1-2-3 took the lead. This program was much easier to use, and brought in even more functionality for accountants. What really helped their workflow was the introduction of macros, which are sets of instructions that could be stitched together to automate common functions. But even that wasn't enough to keep the next generation of spreadsheets from taking over.

Excel

In the mid-1980s, Microsoft launched its Excel spreadsheet, and in so doing turned the tide for spreadsheet software. This is the most commonly used spreadsheet software still, 30 years after its auspicious launch. Accountants, businesses, and households use Excel to create budgets and financial forecasts, record and analyze financial information, create charts and graphs, and keep track of virtually anything from party guest RSVPs to online banking payments to inventory items.

To use programs like Excel to their fullest, accountants developed interconnected spreadsheets that can "carry" numbers from one form to another. That need for flexibility and easy manipulation of numbers and reports eventually gave rise to the all-inclusive accounting software we have today.

AIS HOLDS IT ALL

An accounting information system, or AIS, holds all the information a company needs to stay on top of its finances. The software takes over the many mundane and laborious tasks that used to be done by hand—and use up a lot of paper—in dense transaction ledgers and journals. With that paper system, on-the-fly reporting was impossible; a report request would take hours, if not days, to fulfill. Thanks to automated AIS, though, reporting takes only the time needed to click or tap.

The components of a particular AIS depends somewhat on the business that's using it. Generally speaking, though, a typical AIS will be capable of producing or tracking:

- Check registers
- Invoices from vendors
- Payments to vendors
- Purchase orders
- Sales orders
- Customer invoices

- Customer payments
- Inventory counts
- Payroll data
- General ledgers
- Trial balances

With all of that information, many different reports and statements can be created, including detailed financial statements, budgets, analytical reports, depreciation schedules, and forecasts. In addition, having instant access to the data makes tracking and auditing (verifying accuracy) much easier.

Expanded capabilities and inherent flexibility make AISs valuable business tools, especially for entrepreneurs who like to stay on top of their finances. Now, they don't have to wait for the accountant—or the accounting department—to let them know the state of the business. They can just create a report and instantly see for themselves. But what type of AIS do you need for *your* business?

What Doesn't Belong Here

The AIS holds a lot of information, but not everything. PowerPoint presentations, memos, sales sheets, and the like—even if they include financial data—are not part of a company's recordkeeping for accounting purposes.

SOFTWARE SIZES FROM XS TO XXL

No matter the size of your company, there's an accounting program that will be the right fit. There are prepackaged accounting software tailored to small, one-man-shows; other packages designed for small to midsized companies; and even platforms that work for multinational conglomerates.

Deciding which package is right for a specific company depends on that company's needs and the types of decisions management will need to make. For example, a freelance writer might need just time tracking, client invoicing, and basic financial reporting to feed into her tax return. A mom and pop shop might require robust software that can track inventory, record daily sales, schedule vendor payments, and account for overhead expenses. A department store would need all of those capabilities along with a payroll module; the ability to break inventory, costs, expenses, and sales down by department; and detailed accounts receivable reporting. Basically, bigger and more diverse companies have more complex software needs, and their AIS has to deliver.

Small Companies

Some of the best and most popular prefab accounting programs (available both in the cloud or installed on local computers) for micro (very small companies, like freelancers who don't have a lot of transactions) and small businesses include:

- **Intuit QuickBooks:** Highly rated by a multitude of business owners, QuickBooks is simple to set up and use. In fact, this popular package claims at least 80 percent of the small business financial software market, and for good reason. With it, you can easily import information from other programs, including Microsoft Excel, and export data to tax prep software. You can even connect it with your bank and credit card accounts to simplify accounting for deposits and bill paying.
- **Zoho Books:** Micro-companies don't need a lot of bells and whistles. They just need basic bookkeeping software that can

track their sales and expenses, and output some simple reporting. These features are exactly what you get with Zoho Books. Should your business take off, Zoho offers some advanced tools that let the software grow with the company.

- **FreshBooks:** Designed especially for self-employed people, freelancers, and very small service firms, FreshBooks offers easy to navigate, flexible accounting software in the cloud. The program keeps expenses organized, tracks billable time, and handles client invoicing so you can spend more time working with clients and less time being worried about bookkeeping. FreshBooks also offers one of the best mobile accounting apps currently available, allowing you to check on business finances from any device, anywhere, in seconds.

- **Xero:** Whether your company relies on Macs or PCs for its computing power, Xero has got you covered—and that's a big plus for Mac users who are often stuck with watered-down versions of software originally designed for PCs. Xero's multipurpose program delivers all the accounting functionality small businesses need, automating basic bookkeeping tasks to free up more of your time.

Medium-Sized Companies

Medium-sized companies typically need more than the basic bookkeeping features offered in small business accounting software. Not only do these organizations need more customizable functions, they also need more advanced reporting and analytics. Along with that, these growing businesses need special features like project management and data mining (going through databases to put information together in more pertinent ways). And with many transactions, customers, and vendors to track, they need real computing power. That's why these packages are often referred to as

ERPs—enterprise resource planning systems—rather than simply accounting software. For companies that have outgrown small business status, good ERP choices include:

- **Sage 100c or 300c:** Sage offers accounting software for every business size, and their solutions for mid-sized, growing companies really get the job done. The 100c package unites every aspect of your business, from employees to inventory to compliance issues, and give the option of customizing your system with appropriate add-on modules. The 300c package adds an international twist, making it a great choice for companies with customers outside the United States. Both Sage systems are simple to learn and easy to navigate.
- **NetSuite ERP:** This sophisticated system marries powerful financial management tools with supply chain metrics and production management, seamlessly linking transactions and business planning. This program was created for cutting-edge companies, and allows for international operations and real-time business intelligence for faster, more effective decision making.

Large Companies

Now, there are off-the-rack systems that could work for very large companies. Most of the time, though, corporate giants and multinationals call for customized, proprietary software to meet their specific needs. This customized software allows for specialized transactions, focused internal control and audit features, and particular compliance issues that are too intricate for prepackaged software.

AIS software can be created or tailored to satisfy the specific—and sometimes unique—needs of virtually any type of business. The program then becomes proprietary, meaning the company it's created for (no matter who creates the program) is the only one that can use it.

Sometimes, especially in the largest corporations, an in-house IT department will develop the customized accounting software. They can build it from scratch, or build it up from an existing base program. The main advantage of keeping the program design in-house is access: With direct input from the end users of the software, which includes the people who actually use the accounting program to perform bookkeeping tasks and the people who use it to create reports and analytics, the software developer can make sure it's truly meeting the company's needs.

Specialized accounting software can also be developed by an outside source. If a company goes that route, they should carefully vet the developers they're considering, and call for bids before they decide who to hire. Once that choice is made, the developer will meet with both management and end users to make sure they thoroughly understand the program requirements.

Either way, design is often done in stages, with tons of testing along the way. Since there may be a "language gap" between the developer and the end user, it's very important to involve those users in the testing so as to detect problems and bugs before the software goes live.

SHOULD YOU DIY WITH TAX SOFTWARE?

No matter what the size of your business, you're going to have to pay taxes and, as you've seen, tax law is complicated and confusing. But tax prep software for both personal and business purposes can be very easy to use, especially if you have a relatively simple situation (such as one job, no kids, and no investment or rental income). Doing straightforward tax returns with the kind of software that's available today doesn't take an advanced degree or thorough understanding of legalese. All it takes is organization, time, and patience to do your income taxes yourself. Plus, if you have business income (from free-lancing or consulting, for example), any tax software you purchase will be a deductible expense.

That said, if your tax situation is more complex, you may want to at least consult a tax accountant to make sure you're not paying more taxes than you need to, or setting yourself up to be audited by the IRS. If you do decide to try the DIY route, here are some of the basic factors to consider:

- How user-friendly is the software?
- Is only online software offered or can you download the program?
- Has the online software had security issues, and how secure is the website now?
- How much does the software cost?
- Does it cost extra to fill out a state return, e-file, or include extra schedules?
- Will the program walk you through your return, or simply supply the forms?
- How thorough is the return review?
- What happens if your return gets audited?

Don't just go for what seems like the cheapest software; for one thing, it may have extra costs that pop up as you go, and it may not offer as much flexibility as you need. Whichever program you choose, it will certainly cost less than going to a tax accountant. That said, there are many advantages to using a professional once your financial situation becomes involved. To get you started, here's a look at some robust, proven tax prep software.

TurboTax

There's a reason TurboTax is the most commonly used tax prep software around—it's easy to navigate, supplies a good level of guidance, and lets you directly import tax-related documents from more than a million financial institutions and employers.

H&R Block

H&R Block, the popular "drive-thru" tax prep company, also offers DIY income tax software. Packed with checklists to help you get organized, this tax program smoothly guides you through your return. Its intuitive features offer help—sometimes even before you realize you need it—and supply clear, understandable answers to tax questions.

TaxAct

For budget-conscious taxpayers, TaxAct offers plenty of functionality for a lower price—though it's not as low as it used to be, especially when you tack on state tax returns and extra forms (like a Schedule A for itemized deductions). The program offers summaries of your income and deductions for easier review. In addition, its security features have been amped up (like automatic lockout if you step away from the program for more than a few minutes) in response to a breach in 2016.

ACCOUNTING APPS

Go Figure on the Go

Mobile accounting, which lets you check numbers and run reports at any time from anywhere, is in great demand. This demand has spawned numerous accounting apps that are designed to turn your smartphone or tablet into an accounting information system. Though most of the apps in the accounting categories do basically the same things, each comes with a little twist. All you have to do is find the one best suited to your particular situation.

On the business side, you will want an app that works with your accounting software. This means at least a portion of that software must be cloud-based. On the personal front, there's a lot more flexibility. Your app choice will depend on what kind of information you want at your fingertips, and how security-conscious you are. Here we'll take a look at some of the accounting apps out there so that you can decide which ones might work best for you.

Watch the Wi-Fi

Some phones or tablets automatically connect to Wi-Fi when there's a signal available, and that Wi-Fi often is not secure. Make sure that you do not transmit any sensitive financial information over unsecure Wi-Fi connections.

BUSINESS ON THE GO

Most, if not all, accounting software comes with a related mobile app, allowing quick access to your accounting information from a smartphone or tablet. On top of that, there are apps that let you track and record business expenses, request and accept customer payments, and keep your accounting records more organized.

One of the best mobile bookkeeping apps for small business owners and freelancers comes from FreshBooks. This app helps you create and track invoices, set up recurring invoices for repeat customers, track and organize expenses, create financial statements, and even accept credit cards on your smartphone or tablet. QuickBooks also offers a robust app that connects with its cloud-based software. With a dashboard to help you see imminent tasks at a glance, the QuickBooks app offers full bookkeeping capability and financial reporting on the fly.

Both PayPal and Square let you turn your mobile device into a virtual cash register, easily taking credit card payments and sending the funds straight into the bank account of your choice. Apps like Expensify help you keep track of and organize expenses while you're on the go, either by linking to a credit or debit card, or by taking pictures of individual receipts and letting the app pull out the relevant data.

TRACK YOUR MONEY 24/7

Accounting for your own money usually falls under the category of personal finance, but it's accounting all the same. There are some great apps out there that can help you both track and manage your money through your smartphone or tablet, seamlessly bringing together everything that affects your current financial picture.

Some apps focus primarily on budgeting, others on tracking accounts, and still others on investing and retirement planning. For many people, the most useful are the ones that access the kind of information they need every day to stay on top of their finances.

Here's a quick peek at a few of the best, most popular personal accounting apps currently available.

Money Manager, Budgeting, and Personal Finance

Money Manager, the aptly named personal finance app by Mint.com, takes a comprehensive look at your personal finances, letting you see what you spend, where you can save, and what's going on in all of your accounts. The app helps you create and stick to a budget, and track and manage your money. It even covers loan and retirement accounts. For financial beginners, Money Manager will generate a starter budget based on what you've been spending money on. You can tweak that budget when you have a better handle on your finances. This app is part of the Intuit family, which also includes Quicken, QuickBooks, and TurboTax.

Prosper Daily

Prosper Daily (which used to be BillGuard) offers great credit and debit card tracking. Based on what you use your card for regularly, this app learns and develops a picture of your recurring transactions (like that daily chai latte). On the flip side of that functionality is security, and the app helps protect you from fraudulent charges made on your cards. If the app senses something suspicious, it will alert you right away. The app also offers premium identity theft protection (for an extra fee). Prosper Daily also tracks your credit score so that you can keep an eye on your financial well-being.

Personal Capital Budgeting and Investing

Personal Capital Budgeting and Investing takes a more wealth-building approach to personal accounting. This app offers up easy-to-follow charts and graphs so that you get a very clear picture of exactly where you stand financially. It has the flexibility to track assets by account (for example, everything you have with Fidelity Investments) or by type (such as stocks, bonds, or CDs), and can even track each individual investment separately. You can compare your holdings to major market benchmarks and indexes, which will help you monitor your investment performance. On top of the investing functions, this app lets you track credit cards, set up budgets, and link all of your accounts for quick viewing.

WHAT ABOUT TAX APPS?

Like other accounting and finance programs, income tax return software can now be accessed by an app on your smartphone or tablet. Along with many apps offering guidance, advice, and tax tables, you can now connect with some chain tax preparation companies to share your tax data, or even complete and file your own income tax return using an app.

TurboTax, one of the leading income tax software products, now offers an app that allows users to take a picture of their W-2s, answer some straightforward questions about their situations, and e-file—securely—from their smartphones or tablets. Costs may vary depending on the complexity of your tax return.

Tax prep giant H&R Block now offers an app that lets you import your last year's tax return, upload your W-2, and guides you through the whole process with a simple Q&A approach. You can use as many features (like expert advice and deduction assessments) as you like, and there's no fee charged until you file your return.

Even the IRS has gotten in on the tax app action. The official IRS2Go mobile app lets you check on the status of your refund, locate free tax prep assistance, pay your tax bill, and get free tips from the agency.

ACCOUNTING IN THE CLOUD

Anytime, Everywhere

Mobility means everything today. Everyone wants the information they need at their fingertips, on their phones, in an instant. Business owners, management teams, workers, and accountants are no longer chained to desks in an office. Accountants and clients alike can see information in a variety of forms on demand, no matter where they are; they can even input or update new figures as they happen from anywhere in the world.

Cloud computing has streamlined the transfer of bookkeeping information between businesses and their accountants. Now, as soon as a client posts financial data, the accountant can see the numbers immediately, and view any changes in real-time. As you can imagine, this innovation has greatly boosted accountants' efficiency, and has saved a lot of time and money on both sides.

On top of that, the cloud makes software updates and upgrades easier than ever. In fact, users will hardly notice the changes, as updates are seamlessly integrated into cloud computing activities. Gone are the needs for system shutdowns, reboots, or loading programs on local drives. And if a company decides to change platforms—switching from PC to Mac, for example—their accounting software and data won't be affected at all.

But while there are pros there are also some cons to accounting in the cloud. We'll take a look at both in this entry.

CHANGES FLOW BOTH WAYS

In the past, meetings with the accountant were always on-site, and often required conference room tables where scores, if not hundreds, of documents were spread out. Accountants had to figure out what book-keeping entries needed to be made for financial "housekeeping," and would give a list of those entries to the client to input into their system (or the accounting team would do it for the client, in their offices). Traditionally, this would have taken place only when the accountant came to "close the books" for the period in question. During this process the accountant would have to make accounting adjustments to correct any client errors or prepare adjusting and closing entries. Having the accountant around more frequently could run up a huge tab, straining the budget of small businesses that were too small to have their own bookkeepers on staff.

Some programs, like QuickBooks, adapted to allow the accountant, from his own office, to access and make changes to a client's data. Now, with so much cloud-based capability, accountants who have instant, full access to client data are the rule rather than the exception.

When the accountant needs to make changes or adjustments to a client's records, all he has to do is connect to the information through the cloud. Should the client add or alter information, the accountant is notified, and can check the new data instantaneously. The accountant can also create ad hoc reports, pull information for tax returns (including payroll and sales taxes, along with the company's income taxes), and conduct some review tasks without leaving his office, or poring over pounds of paperwork. Even the arduous task of auditing a client's books no longer requires an accountant to leave his office.

8*JqLn41uM

Complex passwords don't have to be impossible to remember. You can make anything into a hard-to-hack password by changing or adding characters. For example, "mydogbaxter" can be easily transformed into the more complex "mYdo6b@XteR."

SECURITY ISSUES

Cybersecurity is by far the biggest threat to accounting in the cloud. Sensitive and proprietary information, such as employee social security numbers or products in the research and development stages, were traditionally kept under lock and key. Today, even encrypted data can be stolen and deciphered by increasingly tech-savvy criminals.

So how can you secure accounting data in the cloud? The first thing to realize is that it will not be 100 percent guaranteed safe. Nonetheless, there is a lot you can do to make that information as protected as possible. The most important step to take is encryption. For example, before storing files on the cloud, zip them and password protect them. That way only someone with the password can open and view them. You should use long, complicated, passwords, and change them frequently. Also, if you're using a cloud storage service, start by checking their user agreement for information about security protocols, which may include encryption services.

Prior to cloud computing, if your company's computer was stolen, hacked, destroyed, or infected with a virus, you'd lose everything that wasn't backed up—and the vast majority of companies were not vigilant about backing up their information daily. Now, no matter what happens to the physical computer, you can still run your business as usual, because all the data you need is available in the cloud.

And while this innovation is making accounting easier, it really is just the beginning.

TOMORROW'S ACCOUNTING

Where Will We Go from Here?

Where will accounting go next? The industry's future is intimately tied to advances in technology, changing tax laws, and evolving corporate disclosure regulations. In addition, as the world gets ever smaller, and multinational companies are more the rule than the exception, the accounting field will need to develop international expertise to remain relevant.

One thing seems certain: For the foreseeable future, demand for accountants—especially CPAs—will remain strong, with salaries to match.

EVERYBODY WANTS THEM

According to the U.S. Bureau of Labor Statistics (BLS), the demand for accounting professionals is increasing faster than the average for all occupations. Between 2014 and 2024, they project the number of jobs in the accounting field will grow by a whopping 11 percent. Plus, those jobs come with excellent salary prospects. The BLS reported that the current median salary for all accountants (which includes first-year staff accountants and experienced CPAs) is $67,190 per year (as of May 2015). And this agency isn't the only one predicting a rosy future for these financial professionals.

Professional staffing agency Robert Half expects the demand for newly minted accounting professionals to rise for three key reasons:

1. Baby boomers are retiring at a fast pace, leaving accounting firms and companies with accounting departments scrambling to fill their ranks.
2. Financial regulations and requirements are transforming rapidly both in the United States and around the world, calling for accountants to help clients make the necessary changes to remain in compliance.
3. There's a shortage of highly skilled workers (especially in the United States), particularly those workers with technology skills and compliance or regulatory expertise.

IT'S A SMALL WORLD AFTER ALL

There's no way around it: We live in a global economy. American companies have divisions and investments overseas, and shares of U.S. corporations trade on stock exchanges all over the world. On the other side, companies headquartered in other nations have business interests in the United States, and shares of foreign companies trade on the U.S. stock exchanges. As more countries around the world adopt IFRS (International Financial Reporting Standards), the United States may face increased pressure to conform to these common global standards.

All of these factors lead to increased opportunities and demand for accountants, especially those with a comprehensive understanding of global economic factors, cultures and customs, and varying business practices, not to mention strong language skills. Along with those core competencies, a working knowledge of the different tax systems in multiple countries will better serve multinational clients.

SKYNET TAKES OVER ACCOUNTING

Computers and robots are taking over the work world. Factories run on automation, robots help doctors perform surgery, and computers handle customer service calls. The accounting field has been hit along with other professions, as many traditional bookkeeping and accounting tasks are now handled by software.

A Tiny Multinational

A company doesn't have to be a corporate conglomerate to operate in more than one country. With increasing global trade and commerce on the Internet, even very small companies can have a multinational presence.

Though computers have taken over a lot of the technical work, that doesn't eliminate the need for accountants. In fact, it creates a lot of new opportunities. And the truth is that most accountants don't really miss footing columns of numbers or manually posting to ledgers and journals.

Here are just some of the things that accounting professionals can do that computers can't (at least not yet):

- Interpret accounting rules and decide how they apply in a particular circumstance
- Teach workshops that help people take control of their own finances
- Offer strategic advice and implementation services to businesses
- Guide new entrepreneurs through the startup process
- Help clients develop goals and the roadmaps to reach them

- Advise business owners on underlying trends
- Navigate business risks and pitfalls
- Help companies expand and grow at the right pace

There are also many opportunities for accountants that involve taking advantage of the latest technology. For example, CPAs can earn CPE (continuing professional education) credits by attending live webinars, freeing up the time it used to take to travel to and from the classroom. They also can find and complete CPE activities through podcasts, webcasts, and online course offerings.

Advancing technology also provides accountants with new tools and new ways to crunch numbers on the fly to better help their clients gain competitive advantages. With cloud computing, clients have more and better access to their accountants, and the accountants have real-time access to client operations, which increases their ability to stop potential financial problems before they start.

Accountants continue to adapt to changes as they arise, and have done just that since shells and pebbles were used for counting. As software automates the more labor-intensive tasks, and allows clients to do more basic bookkeeping work on their own, accountants can take a big-picture view. And with their experience and insights, accountants have become valuable business partners, helping move companies into profitability and into the future—no longer just sitting in the corner with an adding machine and a pocket protector.

INDEX

ABOUT THE AUTHOR

Michele Cagan, CPA, has worked as a financial planner, accountant, and tax advisor, assisting both individuals and small business owners. She is the author of several personal finance and business books, including *Investing 101, Stock Market 101, The Everything®* *Accounting Book, Streetwise Structuring Your Business, Streetwise Business Plans with CD,* and *Streetwise Incorporating Your Business.* Look her up at MicheleCaganCPA.com and SingleMomCPA.com.